MIND
PLATTER

MIND PLATTER

Najwa Zebian

Andrews McMeel
PUBLISHING®

To the heart in you, don't be afraid to feel.
To the sun in you, don't be afraid to shine.
To the love in you, don't be afraid to heal.

To the ocean in you, don't be afraid to rage.
To the silence in you, don't be afraid to break.

Contents

CONTENTS

CONTENTS

CONTENTS

CONTENTS

Introduction

Of all the gifts I could give you, I choose to give the ones I needed when I was in my darkest moments. You see, we all walk different paths, but there is one tragedy that all of us share: the struggle to be ourselves in a world that wants us to be anything but ourselves.

Here is the gift of understanding when you are in a roomful of people looking right past the pain inside of you.

Here is the gift of *me too* when you feel that you are the only one who thinks and feels the way you do.

Here is the gift of kindness when the world bundles up its heartlessness and throws it at you.

Here is the gift of love when you feel that the only love you deserve is that which others believe you are worthy of.

May these gifts light up your way when darkness overtakes your path. May these gifts allow your true self to emanate from within so that you may be your own light.

Najwa

You Are the Sun

For them to see you shine, you must stay far away, for you are just like the sun; when you're too close, your light makes them blind. And when you're too far, they seek you. So let them seek you. They're getting your light regardless, but appreciating your presence is different from recognizing your existence. If they don't appreciate your presence, they may never even recognize your absence.

Power

Respect the freedom that you were born with but that you've denied yourself. Break free from the power that power has over you and believe in your own beliefs.

Rest Your Heart

Your heart is precious, so take care of it. It may be able to forgive unconditionally, but don't exhaust it by surrounding yourself with those who constantly do you wrong. It may have an infinite capacity for patience, but don't exhaust it by surrounding yourself with those who don't value your time.

Think of Me Too

If you want me to listen to you, respect that I can hear. If you want me to speak to you, respect that I have a voice. If you want me to look at you, respect my ability to see. Do you know how to do that? Listen to me when I talk, talk to me when you hear me, and look at me when I look at you. Share with me not only your sadness but also your happiness. If I can bear hours of your sadness, believe me, it's because I would like to see days of your happiness. Depend on me if you respect that I am worthy of your trust. Open your heart to me if you respect that I am worthy of your love.

Let the Mask Fall Off

I appreciate a genuine effort over a fake attempt to gain my trust.
The clouds overtake the sky for a little while, but the sun always
strikes through.

Stay True to Yourself

Don't worry about what people think of you or about the way they try to make you feel. If people want to see you as a good person, they will. If people want to see you as a bad person, absolutely nothing you do will stop them. Ironically, the more you try to show them your good intentions, the more reason you give them to knock you down. Keep your head up high and be confident in what you do. Be confident in your intentions and keep your eyes ahead instead of wasting your time on those who want to drag you back. Because you can't change people's views, you have to believe that true change for yourself comes from within you, not from anyone else.

Broken Wings

Don't break a bird's wings and then tell it to fly. Don't break a heart and then tell it to love. Don't break a soul and then tell it to be happy. Don't see the worst in a person and expect them to see the best in you. Don't judge people and expect them to stand by your side. Don't play with fire and expect to stay perfectly safe. Life is about giving and taking. You cannot expect to give bad and receive good. You cannot expect to give good and receive bad. Does it happen? Yes, but don't make that an excuse for you to keep doing what you know is wrong. Don't blame life for what you do.

Be Sought

Whatever you do, do it with purpose. Being focused is not something to be ashamed of. It is something to be proud of. When you know what you are doing and have a clear vision of where you are going, you will not need to chase opportunities. Opportunities will seek you. Happiness will chase you. And, instead of being a choice, you will be the one choosing.

Respect Me

Own my heart with your respect. Free me from your deceit.
Captivate me with your honesty. Rid me of your uncertainty.
Challenge me with your thoughts. Enslave me with your
genuineness. Impress me with your spontaneity. Treat me right, and
I will treat you better. Keep me away from what I don't deserve, and
I will bring you closer to what you deserve. Respect me. Be honest
with me. I will give you nothing but multiples of that in return.

Be Considerate

Be considerate of others before you expect them to be considerate of you. Don't freeze time and isolate events in the desire to give yourself the right to blame others for not treating you with whatever you define as *right*. In the grand scheme of things, it is probably your perception that needs to change. Think before you speak, and reap what you sow. Don't ever seek refuge only in people, for if you do, they will fail you sooner or later. But if you seek refuge in and forgiveness from a power much greater than yourself, you will not be turned away, and your eyes will be opened to the *right* right.

Take Responsibility

Don't rely on others to make your life better. You may seem like a puzzle piece that fits nicely into their plans at one point, but what happens if they change their minds? So be it. You have a mind to lead you by logic and a heart to lead you by reason. You choose your fate by taking responsibility and by taking the lead in your life. Don't make yourself part of others' plans. Make your own plan and be part of it.

An Ironic Reward for a Beautiful Heart

Beautiful hearts are hard to find, and to reward them when we do find them, we convince ourselves that they're too good for us. What a reward. Instead of holding on to them, we pull ourselves away. We push them away. We forget that the beauty of their hearts comes from their ability to love and from their willingness to liberate those whose hearts have caged themselves in the past.

Feel Me

I can point you toward the sky, but I can't make you reach for the stars. I can show you the moon, but I can't make you feel its beauty or appreciate its light. I can show you the pathways that you can take, but I can't make you walk down them. I can extend my hand to help you, but I can't make you hold it. I can tell you the truth, but I can't make you believe it. I can tell you how I feel, but I can't make you care.

Lifelong Learning

If you think that education only takes place in an institution, think again. As long as you breathe, your mind, your heart, and your soul are seeking knowledge, so respond to them and nurture their needs. Ask questions and keep your life dynamic. Knowledge is not necessarily confined to a specific subject area. Knowledge is what drives your life and makes it meaningful. So, unless the institution you're referring to is the institution of life, education does not confine itself to the limits of any institution. It extends its wings into every aspect of your life. So, what are you waiting for? Start flying.

Take the Lead

You choose how your life is going to be. Don't let anyone make decisions for you unless they've got your head on their neck and your heart in their chest. Be a leader. A leader of your own life. And don't get yourself to a point where you realize that you are on a road that is not your own. And, no, leadership does not mean that you have to be popular or have people following you. Being a leader is about leading your own mind's logic and leading your heart's reason. Be cognizant of the decisions that your mind and heart make, and your life will be much more meaningful and rewarding.

Change

You can draw a path for your life and have all of your goals set. You can change yourself as much as possible and change things around you just to reach those goals. Here's the catch. Never underestimate the power of fate. It can knock down the highest of goals that seem guaranteed in your life. Plan, yes, and decide, yes, but be prepared for plans not to work. If they don't work despite your hardest efforts, there must be a reason. You may not be able to see the reason at the time, but you will one day, maybe even years later. Did your efforts go to waste? If you don't learn from them, then yes, they did go to waste. Even after changing yourself and your surroundings for the sake of reaching that one goal, you may realize that it was waiting for you at the place where you started, when you were the true you who did not need to change or be changed. Change for yourself, not just for a goal.

Be Honest with Me

Don't tell me what I want to hear. Tell me the truth. It may hurt, but it definitely won't hurt more than the feeling that I was told something out of pity, not out of honesty. If you mean it, say it. If you don't, keep your words until the right person is standing in front of you. If words are said too many times, they become cheap, and I only deserve to hear what is valuable.

The Way They Treat You

Have you ever been told to treat people the way they treat you? Well, don't do that. Treat them better than they treat you. If a person's bad action makes you do the same, how can you say that you are any better? If a person discourages you from doing your own good, encourage him or her to do what's for his or her own good. Remember, you don't have to listen to them, but you also don't have to answer them back in their own tone. If a person disrespects you, react to him or her with respect. Learn from the best. Don't compare yourself by looking down. Always look up to those who struggled yet still inspired their worst enemies.

Simplicity Is the Key

We often fail to see the beauty in the simplest things in life: a smile, a fresh breeze of air, a full moon, a sky full of stars, a simple act of kindness, an inspirational conversation, a childhood memory, a mother's kiss. These are the things that make life beautiful because they will always be there as a reality or a living memory. These simple things do not have a price attached to them, unlike the things we strive for nowadays that we think will make us happy. When we fail to appreciate simplicity, we fail to see and appreciate the most beautiful and important things in our lives. When we fail to appreciate simplicity, we fail at being truly happy.

Reason

Why am I doing what I'm doing? Ask yourself this question when you want to do anything. Diamonds placed in the wrong setting are worth nothing, so if your time and energy are put toward no purpose, you're not moving anywhere. If you're not working toward a real purpose of your own, then you probably are working toward the goal of someone else. Ask yourself, *Why am I doing this?* It's a simple question that can save you valuable time and effort. Don't make spontaneous decisions unless the *why* is spontaneously answered in your heart. The minute you spend to answer that *why* could save you years of wasted time.

Priorities

Hold on to those whom you love very tightly. Love them back, respect them, cherish every moment you spend with them, and make them smile. Do not let a stressful day get in the way of spending the right time the right way on the right people. It's a balance that you can and must strike to make every day worth living. Don't let the day come when you will regret not doing this. Life passes by as quickly as the sun sets and as quickly as the night turns into day. Don't let life pass you by. Fill it with the love that you have in your heart and it will bounce right back.

Care for My Soul

Your soul communicates with the people around you. It sends out signals in different ways, through your eyes, the way you talk, the way you walk, the way you move your hands, even the way you sit. Some people will pick up on those signals and interpret your feelings based on them, or they will not notice any difference. If they do, then they've got the key to your heart. If they don't, then they have much to learn about you. If you can look into my eyes and understand how I feel, then you've got the key to my heart. If you can know that the slightest change in my voice means that I am happy, sad, frustrated, amazed, irritated, or tired, then you are close to me because you are close to my soul and you can understand the way that it is expressing itself. Your soul can communicate with mine, understand mine, and care for mine. Therefore, I will care for yours.

Don't Be Shallow

What is the point of a diamond dangling on a heartless chest? Or on a deaf ear? Or on an ungenerous hand? What is the point of loving people for the way that your eyes see them, not for who they really are on the inside? Don't be the one who gets fooled by an egg dipped in gold. At the first obstacle, its beautiful covering shatters, and all that is left is nothing that will please your eyes. Use your eyes to see into people's hearts, not the way that they make their hearts appear.

Contentment

Have you ever seen a thirsty ocean? Or air grasping for breath? Has it ever seemed that the sky wanted to stretch out more or that the rainbow wanted more colors? Before you ask for something, look at what you already have. Don't ask for more than you need. Don't let your *want* replace your *need*, because a day will come when you will lose what you need to get what you want.

The Power of Silence

Silence can hold more meaning than words. It has power to make a heartless person love and an innocent victim hate. It is much more powerful than words because it takes effort to keep. It is not only about closing your mouth. It is about taking in others' actions or words, thinking about them, formulating an answer, criticizing that answer, searching for logic from your mind and reason from your heart, and then convincing yourself that not saying the answer is better. Silence is not a sign of weakness. It is a sign of intelligence and inner power. It is a sign of faith that replying in the same manner that you were treated will only make you just as ignorant. Learn to be an observer, a deep one, who reflects not only on his or her mistakes but also on the mistakes of others.

Philosophy of Life

I am not better than you because of my religion, color, culture, education, status, wealth, etc. I am not, and neither are you. I must accept, and so should you, that there are differences between us that we were born into. Why do we focus on these differences? Put your hand in mine and let us accept that our differences should not come in the way of us uniting for the basic human values that we share: compassion, peacefulness, respect, honesty, innocence, humbleness, and sympathy. Does a baby born here smile differently than a baby born anywhere else in the world? Do they cry any differently? We may not speak the same language and we may not live the same lifestyle, but a smile I put on my face when I see you puts a smile on your face before you can even think of it. Now, *that* is powerful. I hope that every sense of arrogance or greed in my heart is deviated to a sense of humility, so the wall of ignorance to the real issues in the world can be shattered by the common rights that I share with all of my brothers and sisters in humanity.

Invest Your Feelings Wisely

Be careful what you invest your feelings in, and don't expect people to care for you the same way that you do for them just because common sense says they should. The moment you decide to allow your feelings to move in a certain direction, there is the potential to lose control of them. Your feelings may even become your own enemy through others' hands. That is why I say, don't invest your feelings in things. Don't invest them in people. Don't be good, considerate, honest, generous, and compassionate to others because you are investing in them as people, because you expect something in return. If you do, you will be, and most likely you already have been, brought to deep disappointment. Be good to people because you are investing in goodness, consideration, honesty, generosity, and compassion, because those qualities have never failed to be rewarding. Treat people righteously because you are investing in the righteousness of yourself, and, trust me, you will get something in return. You will be happy. You will be content. You will be truly free.

Forgive and Forget

It amazes me how we always remember how others have wronged us, but we forget how we've wronged others. We always tell ourselves to forgive but never forget. Here is my philosophy: If you want others to forgive you for what you have done wrong to them, then you should do the same. Some people need a second chance. Some people need to forgive themselves for wronging themselves and others. You can be in either situation. We need to help others and ourselves by forgiving others and, yes, by forgetting the actions that they've done as individuals. When you say *never forget*, it shouldn't mean that you will never forget the person doing the mistake but that you will never forget the mistake that was done so that you will remember how it made you feel and never do it to someone else. We are all humans. We all make mistakes. Whether we are courageous and sincere enough to admit that is a different story. If you want a second chance at being the person who you want to be, then give that chance to others. Forgive people, and forget that they have made certain mistakes, but never forget the lessons that you learned from the mistakes they made.

Be Content

At any point in time, we always want to either catch a future event to put it in the present or reach back into our past and change an event, hoping that change will change our present. We don't realize that this moment we are living now was at one point the future that we wanted and will become the past that we may regret not living or appreciating. Before we know it, it's gone, and it's too late to relive it. Why do we always want to change the order of events on our path? Why do we not want to wait for the *reason* part of *everything happens for a reason*? Why do we always want answers at the time we ask questions? We base our happiness on events that may happen in the future: *If this happens, I will be truly happy.* What about now? What about all of the things happening in your life now? Are they really not good? Or just not good enough? Reflect, reflect, reflect. Don't be quick to judge how regretful or amazing your past was, how good or bad your present is, or how great your future will be. Be content with now. Anticipate a *better*, rather than anticipating a *good*.

Be True to Yourself

I may regret many things. Words I said. Words I didn't say. Decisions I made. Decisions I didn't make. Feelings I expressed. Feelings I suppressed. People I listened to. People I confided in. Questions I asked. Answers I gave. Promises I made. Promises I believed. People I respected and people I neglected. Reflecting is essential, but regret should not ground you in the past. It should make you grateful that you have a conscious mind that realizes what is right and wrong. It should give you strength to wisely use your present to make your future better. It should free you. If you don't stop judging yourself, putting yourself down, believing that this is as good as you can be, then you've closed doors for yourself before they even appear in front of you. You've become a slave of your past. Don't expect to be who you want to be without being true to yourself and believing in yourself. If you don't believe in yourself, don't expect anyone to believe in you. If you don't see the best in yourself, don't expect anyone to see the best in you. When you close a door, do you turn back and stare at it and say, *I can't leave because this door is still closed in front of me?* Think about it.

Overanalyzing Kindness

I often find myself wondering how people interpret kindness.
Do they consider it a sign of respect? A sign of weakness? A sign
of happiness? A sign of being naive? It's interesting how a good
thing can be interpreted in so many ways other than itself. These
interpretations and analyses are hidden behind our inner need to
justify others' actions toward us, to understand the *why* behind their
actions. They're based on our inner *wants* of what people's purposes
are, so we start *confirming* what we want their purposes to be with
the things that they do. The truth, though, is that there doesn't
always have to be a purpose for people doing the things that they do.
A smile can just be a smile, a conversation can just be a conversation,
and an act of kindness can just be an act of kindness.

The Vicious Cycle of Rudeness

An important lesson that I've had to learn over the years is that, if I respond to people's rudeness to me by mistreating those who care for me, then I have become like those who were rude to me in the first place. What is the point of putting the people who are good to you down because of others putting you down? Isn't it a vicious cycle of people being victims of rudeness? Turn that negative energy that you receive from people into a positive attitude by appreciating the goodness around you. It will bounce back to you and keep you going. A smile is a beautiful human expression, so when you receive it from someone, don't return it with a frown but let your natural humane instinct kick in and smile back.

A Heart That Cannot Feel

It is easier to have eyes that cannot see those who deserve to be seen by you, hands that cannot reach out to those in need of your help, and ears that cannot hear those who deserve to be heard by you. It is easier to hold back from uttering words to those whose hearts can be comforted by your voice, or to deliberately deprive someone of a happiness you know you are capable of giving. It is all easier than having a heart that cannot feel. It is all easier than having a heart that cannot perceive the pain that you may be causing others. It is all easier than having a heart that cannot fear that it might be treated the same way someday by those whose care you think you might deserve but do not receive.

Pamper Your Wishes

When you make a wish, believe that it is going to happen. Put it in
your heart next to passion. Next to honesty to yourself and others.
Next to humility with yourself and others. Next to consideration for
yourself and others. Next to believing in yourself and others. And so
that the wish will be the perfect gift when it is granted to you, wrap
it from the beginning with the bow of hard work and determination.
Don't ever make a wish and leave it, because it will leave you too. If
you can't do anything about it, then start with your heart. Believe that
you are worth that wish coming true so that you can be worthy of it.

Know Your Power

Just as you can't deny that you can feel love and hate, happiness and sadness, anger and ease of mind, or tiredness and relaxation, you can't deny that you have a fate that, sometimes, you can't control. That doesn't mean that it takes control over you. You can't deny that you have words that need to be spoken. You can't deny that you have a choice. You can't deny the ability that you *can say no*. You can't deny the ability that you have the freedom to make a decision and defend it. You can't deny injustice when you see it, unfairness when you feel it, oppression when you witness it. Stop blaming the world around you for wronging you. Take responsibility for the *nos* you could have said but chose not to, the words you could have said but didn't, instead wrapping your mouth with your own hands and remaining silent against what needed to be addressed. Take responsibility for the choices you could have made but restrained yourself from taking.

Dream Wisely

Imagine planting a little tree and anticipating its fruits. Day by day, you give it everything it needs. Similar to what the tree needs to survive is what our dreams need to survive: hope, which spurs from a little event that we build a dream upon, day by day, second by second, waiting for that dream to become a reality. What happens if the tree of hope grows large, yet no fruits are made? What if the fruits are damaged? What if, after all of that hope that you invested, you discover that there was no dream to begin with? Are you then left with a huge hope that you built on your own for nothing? Never be afraid to dream. But be careful not to let the roots of your dream dig too deeply into the ground of hope, unless you have left enough hope to dream again in case the first dream disappoints you. If you allow all of your available hope to go toward one dream, you will have to wait for that dream to wilt, day by day, second by second— just as it grew—and die on its own before you can make another one.

A Dialogue with Myself

So you go on with your daily life, interacting with people for the most part. Once the night settles its darkness upon you with that imaginary breeze tickling your eyelids softly, causing them to helplessly close, all you have is a confrontation with yourself. Are you who you want to be? Are you really who you seem to be? There's no pretending here. It is you having a heart-to-heart with yourself. One thing that we often miss is that, when fooling others, we are only fooling ourselves. We have habits that we would rather live with than get rid of. We have unspoken words that we would rather keep hidden and rest than speak loudly and show a different side of ourselves. If we don't work on changing that hidden side of ourselves, it will surface one day, regardless of how hard we try to hide it. All I'm saying is, before trying to be honest with others, be honest with yourself. Don't be afraid to take risks and say what's in your heart. Don't risk losing what matters because of the fear of disappointment in yourself or in others.

Happiness Is in Your Hands

When people's definitions of happiness differ, the difficulty of reaching that happiness also differs. If happiness means money or status to you, then wait to pursue it, but if it means seeing and appreciating what you have, caring for your family, seeing beauty in the simplest things, then start now. While you are doing that, others will need something to keep them motivated to achieve their shallow goals of money or power. They will envy you for being so happy with so *little*. People may befriend you for an ulterior purpose, smiling back at you when you smile, not out of happiness for your happiness but out of questioning. How can you be so happy? How can they reach that happiness? How can they take that happiness away? That is what greed can do to people. Greed doesn't always have to do with money, and it is even worse when it has to do with happiness because people start building their happiness on the misery of others, and, oh, how hurtful and deceitful that can be. At the end of the day, be thankful for your health and family. Don't let any insignificant things or people get in the way of this aura of happiness that you choose to surround yourself with.

Trust?

How many times have you told yourself, *That's it. I'm never trusting anyone anymore?* Then you go on, you meet new people, and you trust them. Sure enough, eventually you go back to your initial realization that no one is trustworthy. What is the true meaning of trust? We need to evaluate our beliefs and redefine what we consider trust to be. I am sure that, for most people, it means being able to tell someone your secrets, whether they are about you or not, and expecting that they won't reveal them to others. That is called *being able to listen and not repeat what you just heard.* If that is your definition of trust, then the solution is simple. You need to aim to assess your purpose in speaking about yourself or others to anyone but yourself. If someone is not trustworthy because you found out that they repeated something you said, then how many people's words have you repeated without them knowing? Ask yourself, *What is my purpose?* before you say anything that you consider confidential. That really is not the definition of trust. Think about it. Define it in your head. Take time to reflect.

Where Am I?

Sometimes we think that we know what's going on inside of people's hearts and minds and that we are certain of our thoughts. And it makes sense because, based on our experience with them, we think that we know exactly the way they think. As hard as we try to give others the benefit of the doubt, we feel that we need to protect ourselves from their harm by expecting them to be the same as they've been before. That just makes it easier for us to perceive and understand their new actions. It's a safe feeling. The slightest inflection in their voice can have so much meaning behind it. The look they have on their faces as they are saying or asking for something can tell us whether to read into their words or whether to take them just as they are. The truth is that most of us are constantly challenged to be better than we are, and we do try to *fix* our image to be the way that we want it to be seen by those around us. Somewhere along the way of trying different things that we think will help change us, we may be misunderstood to be trying too hard, to be fake, and to be different than what we really are. Compare this to the metamorphosis of a butterfly. Halfway through, it looks nothing like what it ends up being. It is your choice to either stay halfway through or to continue your journey once you start it, to reach that destination of the person you know you can be.

A New Language

If my heart could speak, it would need a whole new language to express the way I feel. If my heart could create a piece of art, artists could not handle the power of its feelings. If my heart could sing, composers would not be able to put together its symphony, the softest ever made. If my heart could smile, it would flutter out of my chest and into my eyes to see the world with a touch of beauty and a hint of joy.

Baby Steps

Today, promise yourself to be the best that you know you can be at whatever you do. Celebrate the little steps and little successes that you have, no matter how small you think they are. No step toward your dreams is too small. Those little steps are like the beginning of the storm of good things that will hit you; starting with the little steps, the raindrops fall slowly and softly. Don't expect to be an expert at whatever you do from day one. Be realistic. Be up for the journey. Prepare yourself for the victory by staying humble about your achievements.

Delusion

I wonder what's worse, disappointment in reality or feeling indifferent about whether reality changes or stays the same. Life never turns its back on you. You turn your back on yourself when you allow every closed door to stop you from moving on to the next one. Sometimes we choose to stand at a closed door and hope that it will somehow open, although that may defy logic and although we may know deep down that no goodness will come from it. We wait. We choose to wait. We choose to have hope, and we're always scared that the door will open the second we walk away. We claim ownership over what we do not have and fear losing it, although it really never was ours. We read too much between the lines of hope that we weave in our own mind's imagination, only to figure out at the end that we have woven a web of fragile hopes upon fragile hopes. And just as with a spider's web, once one thread is broken, the whole web falls apart.

Wholeheartedness

A risk that you take is only genuinely yours when you put your whole heart into it and go for it with your own convictions, not because of pressures from others. A true risk is one that you choose to take with hope that it will be a milestone for the fulfillment of your vision in life. If a risk ends positively, then you've made the right choice, and if it does not end as you hoped it would, that calls for a reflection on your part and an evaluation of the implications for new risks that you take. Either way, you learn a lesson only if you keep in mind that everything you do is a learning experience and never a waste of time. Time is only wasted when it is used for efforts that prove to be disappointing and we only regard that time as a waste. If we change the way we look at the disappointment, and consider it an experience that we can learn from, we add one new thing into the *shape* of our personalities. Sometimes that is just enough to make us realize the importance of spending time on what we neglected while we took that risk. When you focus on forgetting negative experiences instead of taking time to reflect on them and learn from them, you put yourself at the risk of inviting more negativity into your life, because negative thoughts will pile up, and every time you have a negative experience, you will recall all of the other times and reassure yourself that you have a bad life or bad luck. But when you learn to twist each negative event into a positive lesson and apply that lesson into your new experiences, you become more skillful at seeing the positives in life rather than the negatives. Instead of falling back on all of the *bad* things that have happened to you, you are building a good, positive bank of experiences that has, at its base, the understanding that *mistake* is too big and too negative of a word, while *experience* is bigger and more constructive to your life.

Free

The stars may be too far for my reach, but I am just as far from them as they are from me. It amazes me how the world seems to move in one direction sometimes. There always has to be a start and an end. You always have to be moving somewhere because, if you're not, you might lose the race. The one with the most power wins. The one in the right position wins. The one who is better at playing the game wins. It doesn't matter if you're right or wrong, or if you're trying or not. If you're not good at playing the game, you lose. Before you believe that, ask yourself if the games that you are playing are worth playing and if the races that you are running are worth running.

We Are in This Together

When you're going through a rough time, keep this in mind: Every person on earth has problems of his or her own, young or old, wealthy or poor, healthy or sick. You may look around and see happy faces. You may look around and see that everyone else's life is perfect because they have what they want or what you wish you had. Do you realize that that's how people look at you too? Do you realize that, to some people, you may seem like the happiest person on earth, with the most perfect life? You may be feeling like you're living in a blur. You may not care about how you interact with those around you because you're so engulfed in your own troubles. You may think that they don't even care about how you treat them because they're already happy. What difference is your smile or nice gesture going to make, right? Wrong. You may not be strong enough to draw a smile on your face when you're troubled, but others are. Their troubles may be bigger than yours, worse than yours, and more hurtful than yours. Just because they don't talk about them doesn't mean they don't exist. So, before you look at others and assume things about their lives, or judge them for doing the things that they do, think of how they could be looking at your life and thinking the same. Once you accept this fact, life becomes on your side. Happiness will seep through the broken pieces of your soul, and contentment will sew the pieces back together.

Through Their Eyes

See yourself through the eyes of those who love you. They see all of the goodness in you when you fail to see it. They see the best in you when you see the worst. They are always ready to lift you up even before you fall down. They see every reason why you deserve happiness, love, and joy when you may feel that you're the furthest from deserving all of that goodness. Learn to care about those who care about you before you try to make those who don't even notice you turn your way.

The Journey

Sometimes it's more important to figure out where you are than to decide where you're going. If you don't know where you are, how do you expect to know your destination? We often rush to our next goal, forgetting what we are leaving behind, forgetting those we are leaving behind. We forget that happiness is a journey, not a destination. We forget that tomorrow would not exist without today, and that today would not be what it is without who we are and what we have.

The Heart's Aches

Could it be that you have fallen in love with the unknown? Ask me, as I have fallen way too deep. Could it be that you miss a place you've never been? Or that your fate sends a calming feeling to your heart telling it that happiness is coming its way? Could it be that your heart smiles before your eyes do? Or that you shine just like a star in someone's sky? In a different world, in a different place, oceans away yet skies too close, a heart of gold may be waiting for the perfect moment to flutter your heart with the happiness of your dreams. One day, you will understand what you haven't heard yet and hear what hasn't been said yet. One day, you will hear silence and read what hasn't been written yet.

Happiness Perfected

There are moments when perfection stands in time and space, when the beauty of the moment does not need to be explained, because no words are strong enough. Those are the most beautiful moments in life. When the sunset meets the sea, when the raindrops meet the thirsty crusts of the earth, when the waves hug the shore, when the storm ends and the rainbow begins, when a baby smiles or holds your hand. When beauty meets modesty, when humbleness meets sincerity, when sadness meets empathy, when happiness meets genuineness. Those moments cannot be re-created. They cannot be equated with a price, and neither can happiness. So if you took your happiness from those moments, could you even try to put a price on it? Would you even try to get your happiness from things that are sold and bought? Would it even be possible for you to love people for what they have rather than for who they truly are?

Let Me Be Your Weakness

You are the weakness of those who love you. When they look at you, they see past your face. They feel greatness standing in front of them. They see happiness that they feel they don't deserve. They are willing to stand aside and see you shine rather than risk standing by your side, because they feel that they just might not give you the happiness that you deserve. Admire those who respect you even though they know how forgiving you'd be if they didn't. Those deserving of your love don't take advantage of your ability to forgive because they know how hard it is to forget. Admire those who are kind to you even though they know that you would make an excuse for them if they didn't. Those who love you don't take advantage of your innocence because they know how hard it is to maintain a pure heart in a dark world. I admire those who strengthen me even though they know my weaknesses. I admire those who acknowledge my presence even when I feel invisible, because those are the ones who will understand my silence when I feel that my words are choking on disappointment. I admire those who see me as different, but I love those who see me as unique.

Too Proud

I may be too proud to tell you how I feel or that I need your care. I may be too proud to express how much it means to me that you are doing well and that you are happy. I admit that I am too proud to admit that I have feelings. The thing is, people only see extremes. So, I would rather seem arrogant than needy, although I am not needy. I would rather seem strong than desperate, although I am not desperate. I just want to be content, so I don't want to ask for more. I just want to be happy. If I ask you to care, your care will only be a compliment. It will not be genuine. If I ask you to respect me, your respect will seem like a burden to you. If I ask you to love me, your love will be out of pity. I will keep my pride, and you continue to be blind. But you should know that life is always easier for the one who's loved because all he or she has to do is love back instead of fall in love with the unknown. Life is always easier for the one who is cared for because all he or she has to do is care back instead of care unconditionally. I made my decision to take a risk. Now you make yours.

Childhood Nostalgia

As a child, you usually make decisions without thinking of the
consequences. You just think of the result that you're going to get.
Before you jump, you don't think of the fall, but you think of where
it'll get you. You don't care who's watching, or what they will think.
Before you speak, you don't think of who's listening other than the
person you're talking to. You don't know what judging means. You
make spontaneous decisions, often about going for the things that
will give you instant happiness and moving away from the things
that cause you any kind of stress. I want to be a child again. I want
to jump and fall a million times. I want to not care about what
anyone thinks as long as I am happy with my decisions. I want to be
a child again. My dear self, please let me be a child again.

Questions Unanswered

The questions that you have may be too long, too complicated, or just confusing. A mighty ship lost in the ocean may be stuck in troubled waters, calm on some days and raging on others. So are we in times of hardships and in times of uncertainty. We feel trapped when no trap can contain the amount of agony that we have. We feel our hearts caged when no cage can contain the amount of heartache that we have. Happiness and sadness swing us between the shores of anger and forgiveness. Our hearts may ache for an answer, but the truth is, the lack of an answer is sometimes better than the presence of a lie.

Be a Treasure

Treasures are sought because they are unique. They are different. They are timeless, despite the time that passes after they come to existence. They are not easily found because, to get to them, one must work hard. One must dig deep. One must appreciate the value at hand. You are deep. You are valuable. So let others dig you up.

It's Time to Change

The first obstacle to change is feeling the need to give those around you an excuse. You don't have to explain, but it's okay if you do. Most likely, it is those around you who have made you realize that you need to change, so why would you explain? Would you explain to someone why you're watering a withering flower? Would you explain why you're feeding a hungry person? Would you explain why you're breathing? You don't need to explain why you're protecting your soul from harm. You really don't.

Want Me

Don't tell me there's no place for innocent hearts in this world. Don't tell me I need to accept what I don't believe in. I respect it. Don't confuse my values for my stubbornness, although I am stubborn. Don't confuse my positive attitude for being naive. Allow me to wrap my heart around you for a moment. Listen to this. Innocent hearts may not belong anywhere in this world, but they are big enough for any heart in this world. Innocent hearts belong in innocent hearts. Innocent hearts belong in the hearts of those who genuinely want happiness.

Lead Your Heart

Don't tell me to follow my heart. My heart is innocent. The world is not. My heart sees the best in people when that best might not exist. My heart beats to hopeless hope, flutters to dishonest promises, and sings to unwritten tunes of fake melodies. As it pumps clean blood through my veins, it takes in every impurity aimed at it from the darkness of the world and turns it into a pure thought, a pure smile, or a beautiful lesson. Don't tell me to follow my heart, for following my heart will burn me. Just as a butterfly's aching for light can burn its wings, my heart's aching for happiness might stop it from beating. I want to lead my heart to the harbor of safety. I want the reality that my mind sees, not the reality that it wants, to lead my heart. I want my heart to be just like air: felt, although it cannot be seen, and essential to the existence of another, although its love cannot be contained.

Follow Your Soul

No one knows what you need to do more than you do. Cry when you need to. It's relieving. Laugh when you need to. It's healing. Sit alone when you need to. It's necessary. Surround yourself with strangers when you need to. It's eye-opening. Living by your needs is not easy. No one said it was. But a fact that you should always remember is this: You are more worthy of being taken care of than anyone around you. And I don't mean the superficial kind of care. I mean the care that your soul needs. Everyone around you is struggling somehow. Everyone around you is trying to reach a goal, a destination, or a dream. Just as you might not expose your worries to the world, no one else has to. Remember that you are a work in progress. You are not perfect. You are not expected to be. Do not allow the fear of falling to stop you from jumping. Do not allow the fear of responsibility to stop you from committing. Do not allow the fear of exposure to stop you from shining.

My Philosophy

I cannot count the number of times I've been told not to be too nice to people because it will hurt me. After giving this much thought, my response is simple. When I'm too nice because I have a hidden purpose, others have the right to hurt me, because people are not made to be used but to be loved and respected. When I'm nice for the sake of actually caring about others, and living by my values, then no matter what others' responses are, they can't hurt me. I tell myself that I am being kind to the world, not specific people. Be content with yourself and always smile. If the world smiles back, that's great. If it doesn't, then that's great too, because despite the harshness around you, you are still able to stick to your beliefs, values, and character with a genuine smile.

Break Free from the Illusion of Power

The realities that we are forced to accept in life are sometimes very challenging. Most people will tell you that you need to accept the good and the bad and just be quiet, as long as you're not harmed, as long as accepting and being silent keeps you in your place or moves you forward instead of taking away from what you already have. It is sad but true. We are faced with people daily who tell us that patience is suffering in silence. We are faced with people daily who tell us that following is better than leading and that obeying orders is better than questioning those orders. They disregard the fact that questioning someone's orders or opinions is not a disrespectful act toward those individuals. My philosophy in life and my beliefs request of me to respect myself before I respect anyone else, because if respecting someone else jeopardizes my own respect, then that respect is superficial, invalid, and insincere. My beliefs force me to question everything that comes my way, regardless of where it comes from.

Hollow Hopes

We often build hopes and dreams on assumptions created by our own minds. We design these hopes and dreams exactly the way we desire them to be. They become part of us, part of our own identity, because we authentically created them. An assumption based on something that we aspire to spurs an idea or question in the mind, and after that, every event that happens serves to either confirm or disprove that assumption. Most times, events will confirm our assumptions, not because they are clear but because they don't blatantly disprove them. Our default belief is that our assumption was real. Although this defies logic, realistically, it is a logical sequence of steps that our minds go through. Our minds draw illusions of things we love to see, and our ears hear what we would love to hear. We love the feeling of instant gratification that we get from proving our thoughts. The truth is, a million proofs of confirmation, and a million proofs of disproof, are easier than one *maybe*. Maybe yes. Maybe no. That is why we like our questions to be answered, no matter what the answer is. And, it is easier for our minds and hearts to answer with a yes than with a no because our natural instinct will push us to avoid the disappointment of a no.

Common Sense?

We often forget that common sense isn't always good sense. We conform to what those around us expect, what they consider to be right or wrong, what they consider to be a duty or a privilege, what they consider to be better or worse. We accept the way that people are ranked, as if people were made to be put in some kind of order based on a set of predetermined criteria. Beauty. Money. Power. Status. Appealing, aren't they? We automatically make ourselves followers of and believers in such ranks. We even place ourselves as better than some people and worse than others. Why? Because we are living proof that this way of thinking works. So what do we do? We make a choice to either make our minds follow or lead. Most of us stay in the middle. We recognize what is morally wrong, but we wait for someone brave, someone not afraid to speak up and verbalize what is wrong, and we follow that person. Instead of following the lead of our minds, we follow the lead of people. We forget that a true leader is one who aspires to make those around him think critically and perceive the world with an open mind. To honor a true leader, you don't follow them; you show them that their philosophies and actions encouraged you to free your mind to think. When a leader that we blindly follow makes a mistake, we love being able to blame them for leading us to a *dead end*. We make ourselves slaves to others' beliefs, make our eyes blind, cuff our hands, and nullify our ability to think, judge, silence our hearts, and follow. Then, we blame others for ending up with us at the wrong place. It doesn't make sense. Does it?

Dreams Unfinished

The nature of life makes it inevitable for people's paths and journeys to cross. So, unless you're willing to be the source of disappointment for someone, don't rush to start a plan and then leave it for time to complete. It will become a burden more than a goal. Yes, time helps, but only if you use it. Waiting and passing time is a waste. Instead of starting, waiting, and then completing, you should wait for the right time, then start and complete. Don't open a door you know you can't close, and don't open a door without walking through it. Don't let the fear of the unknown stop you from taking a step toward it. If you're not up for the challenges that may come your way in reaching that goal of yours, then simply don't pursue it. If you're not willing to put forward whatever it takes to reach your goal, then don't aim for it. I am not saying that ends justify means. All I'm saying is, if you don't have the willpower to take the steps that you need to reach that end, don't put your means to use and don't waste your time and others'. If you ignite a fire that you're not willing to contain, the amount of harm it can cause can't be measured, and most times it can't be reversed.

No One's Watching

Would you do all of the things that you normally do if you knew that no one was watching? When was the last time you did something good, without anyone knowing about it, and felt like you'd accomplished something? We tend to wait for people to praise us for the things that we do so we can feel that there was a value for what we did. We add meaning to what we do through the way that we know people will perceive it, and this is relative. It is relative to who we are trying to impress, at which time, and for what purpose. It is an innate drive that makes us want to be perceived in the most positive way by those who appeal most to us, or those who have the power to have an impact in our lives. It is not wrong to want to be perceived in a good way. We all want to be good people. But, this becomes problematic when that praise that we receive becomes the purpose of what we do. Instead of wanting to do good things because of the goodness in our hearts, we want to do good things because we want to impress others, to seem better than others, or even to compete with others. When we have sincere intentions, nothing can stand in the way of us feeling happy and content with what we do. The beautiful part is that the rays of a shining light will eventually penetrate through the darkest of nights, and people will see how truly good you are without you going out of your way to prove it. Some of the most beautiful plants have their beginnings unnoticed under rocks, but that only makes them stronger. If the goal of the sun was to impress us with its light, it would rise when we wake up and set after we sleep.

An Enigmatic Feeling

Once you feel any kind of feeling once, it lives forever somewhere in your heart. It can come and go and become stronger or weaker. Whether it be a feeling of love, hatred, dislike, contentment, disappointment, gratefulness, anger, etc., one truth holds: The more you contain a feeling, the more power it has within you. This is where you have a choice: You either master that feeling or make it become your master. If you master it, your response will most likely be logical, and your actions will be planned. If you let it master you, you may end up doing spontaneous things that may seem to be heart driven. We sometimes have feelings that are so powerful that they can stop us from saying what's right or encourage us to say what's wrong. People choose to deal with their feelings in different ways: talking, art, music, writing, etc. A very common way that we think we can express our feelings is talking. What we miss, though, is that once a word is said, it dies. That's it; it's out of your control now. Whether it be good or bad, once verbalized, part of your feeling becomes placed in the hands of others. For those with a conscious mind, expressing feelings is a red line because it grants others power into our hearts. Because of that, how often do we hold back from saying the way we really feel to those around us? At these points, we should reflect on the reason for holding back. Is it because of the uncertainty attached to those feelings, or is it just that we refuse to sentence our feelings to words that will not do these feelings any justice?

Be the Master

Are you brave enough to be honest with yourself? Are you brave enough to break that wall between your heart and your mind? Your reason and your logic? Your strengths and your weaknesses? Your confidence and your uncertainty? Your beliefs and the way you act upon them? Are you brave enough to admit to yourself that all of those seemingly contradictory parts of you are actually connected? And that their existence depends on you? One does not exist without the other. No one is perfect; we all have a problem striking a balance between these forces within us. Some of us deal with them by surrendering to one over the other. Some of us blame others for strengthening the negatives and weakening the positives within us. Some of us blame ourselves for that. People deal differently with the interaction of these pulling forces within them. At the end of the day, if we are unable to realize that we have control over our feelings and thoughts, and not the opposite, we cannot master them. Mastery gives us confidence, and confidence gives us motivation to move on to pursue our dreams. When you are aware of your strengths and can admit to yourself that you have them because of the hard work that you've done, you can put them to good use. When you are aware of your weaknesses and can admit that you cannot be perfect, you can work on mastering them by avoiding situations in which they are in jeopardy of intervening. Be the master of your thoughts and your feelings and notice the ease with which you can make your decisions, big or small, knowing that you are the one in control of yourself. Don't linger in uncertainty somewhere in the middle.

Know Yourself

Have that wise instinct of knowing how you would react in certain situations before they happen so that you can be well prepared to react wisely. Notice patterns in your behavior, and the way you react in unexpected situations, so that you may prepare yourself to react better the next time. Once you master yourself, *impossible* will no longer stand in the way of your dreams.

Don't Make Me Wait

I breathe honesty, and although I love the feeling of anticipating things, I am too impatient to wait for the truth to be said. The truth can be seen, but it is not believed until it is openly said. I am impatient to wait for the truth because I am scared of losing it before I hear it. How can you be scared of losing something that you don't have? When you can see the truth with your heart, you feel that you already have it. Some moments are made for certain words to be said. We anticipate those moments and build hopes on them. Once we lose those moments, the meaning attached to the words is lost. The meaning attached to what we thought our hearts saw is lost. This is how we lose what we don't have. We believe the truth before hearing it, and we declare ownership over it before we are guaranteed it. Once the moment of truth passes, the readiness within us to hear the truth is lost. The readiness in our hearts and minds to speak back is lost. Now we have an ending in the middle of a story. Before you let a perfect moment pass you by, think whether it is worth your regret afterward for not using it wisely.

The Nature of Life

Imagine sitting outside in the darkness and silence of a starry night, allowing the soft, heavenly breeze of the night to peacefully awaken every cell inside of you. Imagine closing your eyes and just thinking. Imagine thinking and reflecting on where you really are in your life, the purpose of what you are doing, what you want to change, keep, or just stop. Imagine coming to a resolution, changing your intentions, looking at things from a new perspective. It really does make a difference to do that. Now back to reality. In the rush of life, we easily get preoccupied with and fixated on the ideal of where we, as individuals void of anyone or anything else, want to be. That becomes our priority. Everything and everyone else is blurred out and becomes a *waste of time*, as if we don't have duties and commitments toward anyone but ourselves. How do we differentiate between what is and what is not a waste of time? It is relative. The definition of time itself changes from one person to the next. If you're an artist, time spent not painting may seem like a waste of time. If you're a writer, time spent not writing or wandering off into imagination may seem like a waste of time. If you're a mother, time spent away from your kids may seem like a waste of time, or the other way around. The problem is that we get so caught up in life, so caught up in moving toward that ideal that we had planned originally but forgot about, that we can lose track of what really is worth our time and what is not. Along this track, we may hurt those who have no fault in the way that we defined our time. We may even never realize it. If we don't reflect, we may lose those who are precious, only to realize their significance after they're gone, when it's too late. So, next time you perceive spending time with your family as a waste of time, think twice. Next time you perceive sitting alone and allowing your thoughts to wander through the walks of life, think twice. Next time you think that those who love you will always be understanding and will bear the countless hours you spend on others, think twice.

Blurry Lines

Don't confuse someone's niceness with a hidden agenda, and don't confuse someone's meanness with a deficiency in yourself. We were born with an innate love for goodness and seeing happiness around us. As we grow older, we learn that the more we make the happiness we are willing to offer hard to get, the more satisfied we will be. In my opinion, being sincere, regardless of the consequences, is a billion times better than pretending to be someone you're not, regardless of the rewards. Don't take advantage of your abilities for the sake of achieving power. Don't confuse power with control. Don't confuse what you want with what you need. Don't let your inner voices alter the reality of what you see. Be confident, logical, and reasonable. Don't ever deny that you need to change the way you look at things before you change the way things are. In a desert, you can see an illusion of water partly because of your thirst, but that doesn't mean that it exists.

New Chances

I don't believe in putting up walls built by those who hurt you, in the face of those who you don't even know yet. How can you expect someone to break down a wall they never built? Despite the seemingly painful importance of having a positive outlook toward new people, tainted by the hardships that others have forced you to go through, you have to always be open to the idea that people are not all the same. People can change for the better. If it weren't for hope, would we have the capacity to live? We all meet people who belittle us, but we often forget that it is not because we are not worthy of their respect but because part of them does not allow them to accept seeing goodness in others. When belittled for no reason, be confident that it is because you've done something right that others cannot allow themselves to admit to. They need help, not you. When you meet new people, you need to be able to ignore all the nagging whispers of your heart and mind that remind you of all of those who have hurt, used, and disappointed you. If you let those thoughts get to you, misleading you into expecting the worst in people, your reaction to them may make them think that you are belittling them. Does that make you think of all the people you thought had bad intentions toward you but who really had only been hurt by someone before, who thus expected the worst in you, and who mistreated you based on that?

Silver Lining

Have you ever been told not to show others your happiness or the good things that have come your way because they might envy you? Don't worry about those who cannot be happy for you, who cannot see the beauty within you. Beauty from within allows you to see goodness in others. It makes you see beauty in the simplest of things, to be content and to appreciate what you have before you ask for more, to value the moment you live in, and to hope for others in the same way that you hope for yourself. It allows you to forgive and forget at the same time that you learn. It allows you to be positive, to be optimistic, to see that silver lining even before you see the cloud. Everyone has this beauty, but it exists along with other characteristics, which may be in an imbalance at times: envy, hatred, pessimism, ungratefulness, discontent, jealousy, etc. Unfortunately, those characteristics will make others attribute your success and happiness to the things that you have, to the superficial things in your life, instead of looking and actually seeing the real you. People have a difficulty admitting that you are actually successful because of your hard work or because of your determination. They have a hard time admitting that you actually deserve the happiness that you have, so they are unable to be happy for you. You sometimes give those people a license to affect your feelings, and they use it against you, maybe not intentionally, but they do use it against you one way or another. You think that someone being rude, disappointing, or just plain weird around you is doing so because of something that you've done wrong. That right there is the beauty within you refusing to see that others may actually be responding to those negative characteristics within them. Hold on to that beauty within you and let it prevail over other characteristics because that is what keeps you moving forward while others are busy trying to figure out the *things* that make you happy.

The Quest for Reasons

The answers to some questions in life lie in the absence of an answer. The reasons that we seek, the silver linings that we desperately want to see, the hidden messages that we try to figure out may simply not exist. Or they may, but only if we change the angle from which we look at them. We rush from one stop to another in life, searching for reason, for meaning, for purpose, not realizing that there are certain stops where we must wait if we arrive before our time. We often rush and wait. Although we learn many lessons while waiting, because we have that time to think and reflect, we miss the beauty of the simple things along the way. We miss other opportunities that may have been better than the place where we stopped. We often question why the things that we didn't want to happen, happen, or why the things that we wanted to happen have not happened yet. We fail to be thankful for, or appreciative of, the good things that we did not ask for but that happened anyway. We fail to be thankful for the bad things that we did not ask to be protected against but that did not happen. Our nature is to think more about yesterday and tomorrow than today. We don't realize that today was yesterday's tomorrow and tomorrow's yesterday. We waste our time when we look too far back or too far forward and miss living yesterday's dream today. Then we wonder why our dreams do not come true.

Life, Simplified

Don't ever force yourself to live up to anyone's standards. Make your own standards based on your abilities, based on your potential, and based on your vision for your future. Take time to figure out what the big picture in your life is, what your end goal is. This is personal to you. The conviction in your heart of this vision will make it shadow you wherever you go. It will guide your every step, decision, and plan. No one is more knowledgeable of the real you more than you are knowledgeable of yourself. So, why let others dictate what works and does not work for you? Do not settle for the label *average* or think that you are no different than those around you. Be the phenomenal person that you know you can be. Define *phenomenal* yourself. Don't compare yourself to anyone else's *phenomenal*. At all. You don't live in people's hearts to know who they really are. Don't think that you deserve any less than what you have or that you don't deserve any better. Don't seek the acceptance of people who you think are a little better than you just because you want to feel that someone better than you accepted you into their life. What a miserable feeling that would be, to need someone's acceptance to accept yourself. Have your own big dreams and pursue them because you know you can. No one is stopping you from that except yourself. Don't live your whole life comparing yourself to people you think are better than you, trying to live up to them. Live your life working to make who you are today better than who you were yesterday and dreaming that who you will be tomorrow is better than who you are today. Do not give yourself any other option than becoming better. Don't be anything other than positive. Celebrate your little successes and improvements. Imagine how truly happy you will be.

A Wish Come True

Have you ever wished for something so badly, and when you got it, you had doubts about how much you wanted it? Have you thought about something constantly for a long period of time, swung hopelessly between the victorious triumph of achieving it and the desperate misery of being disappointed, while imagining all the things that would happen to your life if that wish were to come true? Why is it that we really start evaluating how much we need something the second we get it? Is it because we think we are not worth it? Is it because we have a change of heart? Is it because it comes a bit too late? Is it because our hope for it runs away, our desperate need for it fades, our wasted time put toward it exceeds the limit that we can bear? Is it because the feeling of gratification that we get from accomplishing what we want, regardless of what it is, is greater than what we want? Is it because the feeling of winning something over takes over the value of the thing itself? Everybody wants to be a winner, and that is not a problem, but what is it that

you want to win? Is it just the feeling of winning? Everybody wants
to feel that he or she is right, worth a wish coming true, worth the
feeling of accomplishment. Once we learn to look deep into our
hearts and deep into our minds, we will learn to want that which we
appreciate before we have it. Why? Because our well-being is in need
of it. If you cannot appreciate what you don't have before you have
it, you will not appreciate it after you have it. Period. We thrive on
the idea of being able to change our surroundings to suit our needs,
and we promise ourselves to change so many things once we finally
get that one wish. But what we ignore is the fact that our hearts and
minds are in need of constant care so that they do not feel the need
to change others for them to be content. I will not tell you to be
careful before wishing for something and allowing yourself to dive
into its beautiful sky of imagination. I will tell you to be careful to
treat yourself well, and to be responsive to the needs of your heart
and mind, so that you may be content with what you have and so
that, if you wish for something, you already know its value because
your heart and mind truly do need it.

A Step Forward

You know those moments when you feel stuck between moving a step forward or staying where you are, comfortable in your own place, not wanting to commit yourself to something more? Those are critical moments that we often shy away from because of the unstoppable chain of questions attached to them: What if I regret this? What if I can get something better if I wait a bit longer? What if it's not really meant for me? What if now is not the right time? etc. Taking certain steps toward your future is one of the toughest things to do because you are afraid of being stuck with something that you can't get out of. You are scared of the unknown. We wish we knew what was coming, yet we love the feeling of something new. We would rather the route of life bestow its action upon us, and accept what it gives us and deal with it, than take the lead and go out to make our own future. We would rather respond to an action than initiate an action ourselves. I do that sometimes too, but I've come to the realization that a decision not made at the right time can affect the course of a lifetime, a suitable commitment not made can change a destiny, and an opportunity for growth not taken can affect our biggest dreams. How do you determine what the right decisions, commitments, and opportunities are? This is where you take the lead. Balance your mind's logic and your heart's reason. Now make a decision, make a commitment, take an opportunity.

Why I Believe

Have you ever looked at the way that someone lives and thought to yourself that it just doesn't make sense? When we are born, we are acculturated into a certain set of beliefs that becomes the *right* way for us to live. It's the life that makes sense to us because that's all we know, and those beliefs become part of our identity. Anything else is new, and we avoid it because it just doesn't feel right. It makes sense to feel that way, doesn't it? You're raised into the beliefs of those who raised you because their beliefs are instilled in them and are echoed in the way they see your life progressing. Here's the catch. Are you able to defend your beliefs? Or do you just say, *That's just the way it is*? You must critically think about everything around you, because if you don't know deep inside the reasons you believe in certain things, you will lose your commitment to them at the first obstacle you come to. You have to be convinced by your beliefs, thoughts, and way of life. Think of the reasons you do what you do and the reasons you accept certain things and reject others. If there are no reasons, then work on finding them. Maybe then you can actually learn to accept that differences among humans exist and that the *right* life is relative. Take the time to evaluate your life. How can you take the lead in your own life if you've already allowed yourself to be a naive follower in it?

The Right Thing

When we say *the right thing at the right time*, it means that the time being right is included in making the thing right. That's why it would not make sense to say *the right thing at the wrong time*; the right thing cannot be right if it's not done at the right time. It is also not right if it is not done the right way or if it does not have the right purpose. Be cautious with the way you do the things that you do. Make sure that you complete a job that you start and realize that completing doesn't always mean that you are stuck with something till the end. It can also mean stopping, but that's the part we usually miss. We usually keep things hanging in space and time. Put your heart into anything you do and put in all of your efforts toward it. If you don't have the motivation for it, then maybe that is not what is meant for you. Stop doing what is not right for you and what does not suit your dreams. Learn from the experience. Start doing what you love, the right way.

The Power of Ownership

Everything that we are is to some extent owned by others. Our words once they are spoken, the way we look once we are seen, the actions we do once we act upon our thoughts. The only thing we have true ownership over is that which cannot be seen or controlled by others. Our thoughts. While a hurricane of thoughts may be going on in your head, you can seem like the calmest person on earth if you know where to draw the line between your thoughts and the extent to which you act upon them. Our thoughts are either translated to actions very early in their development or they lead to bigger and deeper thoughts. They can also be translated into a strengthening power for us. Our strengths lie in the way we are able to control our thoughts and in the way we are able to manage our weaknesses by turning them into strengths. We should not allow others to own the control over our weaknesses, for once we do that, our strengths become slaves to those in control of our weaknesses.

Will You Dare to Ask?

Doubt and uncertainty are probably the two things that keep us from doing half of the things that we think of doing and that we regret not doing later on. Although some things are meant to be and some are not, there is that pressing feeling within us that just wants to know what is meant to be and what is not. While we want to know the answers to some of the burning questions that we have, we often fail to do the simplest thing that we can do to get the answer: ask the question. We don't ask the question. We live with the hope that it will magically answer itself with time, and our excuse is, *If it's meant to be, it will happen.* We would rather it be not answered and kept inside rather than be asked and expose our thoughts. At this point, it is a personal preference. Some people are blunt with their thoughts and will be straight up, and others not. Does that make either wrong or right? No. Does it affect their destinies differently? Yes. There is a difference between avoiding the questions that you have and seeking answers to them.

Don't Lose Track

I don't live in your heart or in your mind, so I cannot judge your intentions or your beliefs. Although your actions may give me a good impression of who you really are as a person, and although I may learn some lessons from your mistakes, I have no right to openly judge you because my purpose in life is not to criticize other people's lives but to be respectful and considerate of them along my own path to reach my end vision in life. My path may cross with yours, and I may believe that you are on the wrong track, but if I lose track of my path because I'm too busy judging yours, I will waste my time and yours. Who I am and what I believe in are mine to keep, and who you are and what you believe in are yours to keep. They are yours to strengthen, change, or even keep the same. As long as we can be true to ourselves, stay away from hypocrisy, and be respectful toward one another, we will be happy along our paths to reach our dreams. One day, you will realize that there is no one more worthy of your attention or your criticism than yourself. Imagine putting all of the effort and energy you spend criticizing others and exposing their mistakes toward bettering yourself. Wouldn't you be much more content and happy?

Broken Promises

If they break the promises that they once made, it does not mean that you were not worth making these promises come true. It means that they are no longer willing to put in the effort to live up to their words. You did your part by believing their words. And that's what good people do. Even if there is a chance the other person is lying, we believe them. Not because we are naive. But because we believe *in* them. We believe in their ability to fulfill the words they have said. We know that it's much easier to give up on someone than it is to make a difference in their lives by being someone who believed in them.

Sincerely, My Heart

Just because someone doesn't acknowledge what you do, it does not mean that they don't see it. People are selective in making obvious what they see about you. They may acknowledge it in their hearts but avoid allowing you to see that. They may avoid that simply because they think it's expected of you and not anything that you need praise for. Others will not acknowledge your work because you don't acknowledge theirs. Others won't because they think that you've got enough ego or confidence to the point that you don't need any praise. Some won't simply because they think that even if they did acknowledge your work, you would not notice them. Similarly, some people will acknowledge what you do because they think that you did something that you didn't have to, or because you acknowledge what they do, or because they think that you need praise to realize your potential, or because they want to be noticed by you. Don't evaluate yourself through people's words or through their praise. Let the sincerity in your heart for what you do break through that need within you to want to hear that you've done something right. Let the sincerity in your heart see the sincere acknowledgment in other people's hearts.

Thoughts Unexpressed

There are so many thoughts that would be much more beautiful if they were just kept as thoughts. Words sometimes don't do justice to our thoughts and feelings. They are better kept inside to last awhile rather than said and forgotten. Every thought has the right time to be verbalized, and every feeling has the right time to be expressed. Meanwhile, enjoy the thought, enjoy the feeling, and give them the time they deserve to be as strong as you want them to be.

Goodness Gone Wrong?

When someone you've done so many good things for makes you feel unappreciated, do you, even for a moment, wish that you could take it all back? Do you regret doing good things for the wrong people? Personally, I don't agree with that. At the end of the day, everything you do belongs to you. All of your actions belong to you, whether good or bad, for yourself or for others, intentional or unintentional. Instead of regretting doing something good for the wrong person, it is better to regret taking that time away from those who do good things for you. Don't ever regret a good deed. Ever. As much as it hurts to see that someone does not appreciate your work, your work is really not for them. Your work builds you and your personality. This is where you need to think of your purpose behind anything you do. If your purpose is to please others and look good in their eyes, then you are bound to be disappointed because your pleasure is in their hands, not yours. If your purpose is to truly and sincerely be a good person who spreads a positive and mature attitude that rises above individual needs, then you will be disappointed less often and in a different way. You will be disappointed that someone, regardless of who this person is, could be so blind and ungrateful for something good. You will be disappointed for them, not in them. Think of your purposes and work on yourself. Once we realize that we need to change the way we view the world before we try to change others, our purposes will be geared in the right direction.

Be Sensitive

It irritates me when people actually believe that they are better than others. It irritates me that someone could give him or herself the right to talk down to others or accuse others of doing things without asking for their side of the story. It irritates me when people get pleasure in seeing others fall flat on their faces in pursuit of their dreams. It irritates me when people strive to please and live up to those with money, status, and power. It irritates me when people are more negative than positive and spread their negativity wherever they go. It irritates me when someone does not return a smile. It irritates me when people judge others based on their looks before they even get to know them. It irritates me when people wait for the hidden purpose behind every act of kindness, not realizing that sometimes it just does not exist. It irritates me when I see love given and not returned. Many things irritate me, and I have learned that the way to stop that irritation is not by becoming immune to these things. It's a valuable quality to be able to recognize bad things when you see them and to learn from them. If you have that sensitivity, never let it go. If these things irritate you, work on convincing yourself that you will do what you can and that you can only do so much. At the end of the day, we're all human, and sometimes we cannot extend our helping hands further than they can reach, especially if others are not willing to extend their hands back.

Let Go

We often attach letting go to negativity because we take it as giving up, and giving up is a sign of weakness. That's not always true. Sometimes letting go can be as positive as holding on, and sometimes holding on can be as negative as letting go. Letting go of what makes you miserable is the right decision to make because while one opportunity that you are holding on to makes you cry your heart out, another opportunity is patiently waiting for you. It is patiently waiting for you to let go of what you have and hold on to this new opportunity. When you let go of what you have, do it the right way. Don't let go feeling weak. Don't let go feeling like you've done anything but your absolute best. Don't let go feeling like you were not worth the opportunity. It was not meant to be worth your pain, although it may have been painful. Think deeply into the purpose that made you take that opportunity, and if you've achieved that purpose, then take pride in it. Give yourself credit and don't ever let anybody put you down. Let go feeling like the biggest winner and let loss go home with the opportunity that never appreciated you. Reflect. Learn. Move on. Hold on to the next exciting thing that the world opens up for you and put your best forward, for your best will never let the inner you down. Ever.

Decide

Sometimes life throws at us what we think is more than we can handle. We stress. We complain. We spend more time worrying than working our way through what must get done. We complain if we don't have something and we complain more if we have it. We forget that, for something to be in our lives in the first place, we must have accepted it and decided to let it into our lives. I understand that sometimes you don't have control over what comes into your life, but at that point, you have two choices. You either accept the challenge or deny that it exists. If you accept the challenge, you need to prioritize your list of tasks and see where that challenge ranks and how much time and energy it deserves. Give it that much, no more or less. If you choose to deny its existence, no one is stopping you, but take responsibility for the decision of ignoring it. No one has to deal with your problems. We all have problems of our own to deal with. Whether you take the challenge or leave it, it will exist, and because it was meant for you, no one else can deal with it but you. That's the reality of life. It is the attitude with which we conquer life's challenges so that we live happily. Sometimes the feeling of achieving something is greater than the achievement itself. So, don't take a challenge too personally. Accept that you must deal with it and realize that you can because you've dealt with many challenges before. Remember that there is a reason for its existence, although that reason may be hidden. So, will you choose to face your challenges with a positive attitude? Or will you keep ignoring what you must deal with and pile it on top of everything else that you've been ignoring? Whatever you choose, take responsibility for it, not because you have to but because you can and because you want to. Life never comes against you. The way you deal with it comes against you. Be at peace with yourself and see how many challenges you can take once you give yourself the credit that you deserve for being able to deal with life's most difficult times.

Inspire

If you aim for perfect, you will always be disappointed. Don't expect everyone to be up to your expectations unless you are willing to live up to someone else's. We have to accept that no one is perfect and learn to let go of the mentality that people can't change. People are not all born into the same environment, and they are not born with the same definition of what is right and what is wrong. What we see as someone making a mistake may only be our perception that something is wrong. Their perception may be that everything is completely fine. Sometimes all a person needs is to fall once or twice to learn on his or her own. Sometimes all a person needs is to come across those who will inspire him or her to change for themselves. Is it fair that we give up on people because of what they've done in the past? Is it fair that we define people by their past rather than their progress toward their future? Be the person to inspire others to change if you can, and if you can't, then don't destroy them by confining them to what they've done before. Don't set people up for failure by showing them that they're not good enough. When you make others feel that you believe in them and that you believe that they can change for themselves, you will see what a world of a difference you can make.

Transparent Heart

Sometimes people make obvious what's in their hearts, not necessarily through words but indirectly through their actions. Do we make what's in our hearts as obvious in return? Sometimes we try so hard to hide our thoughts and feelings because we are scared of the unknown. We are scared that, once our thoughts and feelings are exposed, they will not be taken care of by others the way we took care of them for so long. We are scared of letting go of what is in our control and putting it in someone else's hands. We take a step ahead, and because of that fear, we take ten steps backward, not realizing that we are causing that same fear for others. We are scared of being misunderstood. And because of this, we linger in a state of uncertainty, not knowing what to do because all we know is what we see and not what we hear. Although feelings are much stronger than words, it somehow brings ease to our hearts and minds to hear what we would like to hear before we can let go of that fear. We forget that, sometimes, simply saying what needs to be said can make any trace of uncertainty in others turn into a confidence that cannot be defeated.

Intuition

Sometimes we just know what to do. We have a feeling that it's right, and so we do it without having an intended or obvious reason for it. But the reason does exist, and our feeling is valid, pointing in the right direction. For perfectionists like myself, it's hard to attempt anything that does not have a valid or clear reason and that comes in the way of us taking risks or following our gut feeling. That's because it feels like taking directions while being blindfolded, unable to see the end that we are walking toward. So, when we do allow our intuition to take over, we feel that we are taking a big risk and that we are trusting others to lead our way, and that's when every small step seems like a journey. Every small step requires so much effort and so much courage to take. We need to get a positive response after every small step because, without that, we feel discouraged and want to go back to the start, where we were in ownership of our path. We did not have to trust anyone but ourselves. We did not have to walk toward the unknown. We did not have to feel that we were wronging ourselves by giving into what we felt, instead of what we thought. It's our safe place. But the beauty in allowing our intuition to take over sometimes is in the possibility of it leading us to the right place at the end, where we realize the reason for what we did.

Mature Decisions

I don't like this attitude of people who decide that being alone is better than being around others just because others hurt them. If you consider yourself a considerate person who has been wronged by others, then, trust me, there are people just like you. You just are not seeing them, and that makes you just like those who are hurting you. You have negative people in your life? People who praise those who make them feel like garbage and then make you feel like garbage? People who refuse to support you when you need it most? So tell me this, why are you keeping them in your life? There comes a point when you need to eliminate some people from your life, not because you don't believe in their goodness or because you don't think that there is a chance for them to change, but because they do not appreciate you to begin with, and they never did. You were always their sidekick, and once you started shining, they could not handle your success. How are you supposed to inspire them to change if you stay the weak follower that you are? Cleanse your life of cunning people who pretend to care for you when they really don't. If they can't be happy to see you happy, and if they refuse to see your inner beauty and give you credit for who you really are, then why are you giving them a second of your time? Walk away and see if they would ask you to turn back around. Let them realize what they lost.

Believe

Hope for the best and believe that it will happen, and it will happen. If it doesn't, then it wasn't the best for you. There's something better waiting. Before you lose hope, stay positive, see signs in the littlest of things, and move in the direction of what makes you happy. Your heart gravitates toward real happiness, whether it is your definition of happiness or not. Listen to it when you can't find a logical reason not to. Where it takes you is where the best awaits you.

What If

You know those moments when a beautiful *what if* crosses your mind and makes you smile from the core of your heart? The moments when you find yourself lost in a dream, with happiness overwhelming your heart? Those moments are mirrors into the life that you should be living in order to be truly happy. Sometimes we are so preoccupied with just getting by in life that we forget to truly live it, with every meaning of *live* possible. Those are the moments that will allow us to feel meaning in what we do. They allow us to enjoy our time while doing what we love. Those are the moments that make the happiness in our hearts shine into the hearts of others. Those moments are the extensions of one single event that springs hope into our hearts and spurs an imagination of our future right before our eyes. Whether we make that imagination true or not depends on whether we take a step toward it. It's in our hands. You may not be able to get there on your own because others need to put their hands in too, but do your part and live knowing that you tried. Do not spend your life wondering about what could have been after the light that was present to lead your way was dimmed by the *life* you thought you were living.

A Battle to Win

The faces that we wear in different environments can tell a lot about our personalities. Do you find yourself speaking differently when you're around different people? Do you care more about what you say and how you look in front of certain people and not others? Do you put more effort into thinking of the words that you say or the things that you do in front of certain people and not others? It's interesting to be aware of these differences within you that you may not be conscious of. The real challenge is when all of these faces or personalities come in confrontation with each other in order to determine which one is really representative of you. Which one do you feel most comfortable in? Which one do you put yourself in when you want to impress others? And when you meet new people who know nothing about you, do you create a whole new personality based on what you learned from your experiences in all the other ones? How much effort do you make to put yourself in each one? The bottom line is if all of those personalities or faces that you have are not at peace with one another, and if they have any major differences, then you are still uncertain of your beliefs and of who you really are or who you want to be for the rest of your life. So, what are you waiting for? Don't wait until others pick up on your contradictions and confront you about them. Take a break and deal with your issues before you worry about dealing with the issues of others. This is the time to put yourself first and try to bring all of the contradictions within you to a halt. The sooner you have this confrontation with yourself, the sooner you can be comfortable with yourself. After you reach a consensus with yourself, your genuineness will shine upon every single person you meet without you trying. So go ahead, let that battle within you take place until you become at peace with yourself. After that, you will feel the true confidence in yourself that you've always longed for. Go ahead and start.

Contemplating Happiness

Survival is not the same as living. Smiling is not the same as laughing your heart out. Thinking is not the same as having a deep conversation. Listening is not the same as really caring. Words are nothing if they are not spoken, and feelings are doomed to be erased if they are not expressed at the right time. Sometimes we are afraid of taking that extra step that takes us from what is ordinary to what is extraordinary, that extra step toward really being happy, because happiness seems just too good to be true. It seems too far away to dream of. It seems too hard to get, too hopeless, too risky. But what's the point of realizing the extraordinary if you don't go for it? You're better off not realizing it and living a content life rather than realizing it and feeling hopeless about it. There is nothing wrong with what's ordinary, but if extraordinary chances come your way, let the happiness that your heart desires extend out and reach for them.

Listen to Your Heart

Once you realize that life is not perfect, you truly begin to live a beautiful life because beauty is in comparison with everything else that is less than it. If life were perfect, we would all live the same life, and we would not have unique experiences. We would not need *better* and *best* because everything would be *good*. If life were perfect, opposites would not exist because, upon their existence, perfection would fail to be the same in everyone's eyes. Differences would not exist. We would be objects, not the live souls we are now, souls who aspire to reach perfection while understanding the fact that perfection does not exist as one thing that everyone agrees upon, that it exists differently in the way that each one of us perceives the world, happiness, and contentment.

Disappointed

It is far less disappointing to realize that the characteristics you've come to dislike in people in the past are present in new people than it is to realize that those characteristics are present in yourself.

Between the Lines

We all have this inner need to be stable, the need to feel that we have a place where we belong. We like to gravitate toward what puts our hearts and minds at ease. Everyone wants to be free of any captivating or weakening feelings and thoughts, but ironically, we also like to feel grounded by that which we cannot control. We like to feel that there is a greater power over us, one that sometimes allows us to justify the actions that we do despite logic telling us not to. As much as uncertainty puts us at an unease because we are swinging between the hope of a *yes* and the disappointment of a *no*, we love that hope, that possibility, that *maybe*. We sometimes read nonexistent meanings and feelings between short lines, but we see them because we want to belong, because we want to feel stable. The possibility of their existence forcefully tempts us to see them. Depending on the power of uncertainty that we have, if, at the end, we find out that those meanings do exist, we value them more because we have already worked hard for them by foreseeing them and hoping for them. Meanwhile, we have to understand that uncertainty is something that we need, that time is something that we need, in order to really appreciate what we end up getting.

Avoidance

Time passes, the past is inevitably created, and we get moved out of it into the present, but do we really move past it? Avoid a nagging thought or feeling for a minute and see how many days it will take you to deal with it in the future. The main reason why we live most of our lives recalling the past is that we don't really get rid of it. We keep unresolved problems in it, and that makes us visit it often to deal with them. Feelings and thoughts that we ignored at the time that we were able to control become too complicated once the issue shifts from *How do I deal with this?* to *Where do I even start?* We are good at avoiding. We are good at just disappearing because we think that if we stay away from a thought or a feeling long enough, it will just go away. Meanwhile, the complete opposite happens because, subconsciously, your need to deal with the issue becomes more persistent. That need for resolution becomes stronger. Taking time to understand why certain thoughts cross your mind, and what you need to do with them, is absolutely critical, and conviction of your decisions is even more critical. It is always better to be at peace with your mind and heart so that you lead the directions that they take. Otherwise, you will find yourself acting in ways that even you don't understand.

The Language of Silence

There's something about silence in others that we find frustrating yet intriguing. When you are faced with silence, you have the ability to interpret it in whatever way you want. It's very interesting because silence is not a language, yet it could be more powerful than any language, and it is present absolutely everywhere. It may seem that it doesn't take any energy, but it actually can take more energy than speaking because you hold yourself back from saying what you want to say. We use it to convey happiness, sadness, acceptance, deep thought, disappointment, inability to express our thoughts and feelings, or even carelessness, etc. Sometimes we use it unintentionally, and we are unaware of how those around us interpret it. When speaking words, we can change what they mean by simply changing our tone, but silence has no tone. Instead, the silence of another person awakens many voices within us: those that will tell us what we want to hear, those that will tell us exactly what we need to hear, those that will tell us what we know that we deserve to hear, those that will tell us to wonder about what would happen if that silence meant this or that, etc. This is where our original intention kicks in, and based on it, we have this self-talk that makes us feel shame, guilt, pride, conviction, disappointment, etc. So think about it. Do you actively and selectively use silence as a form of communication? Do you ever think about how people around you interpret it? Similarly, do you give the silence of others the attention and thought that it needs? Or do you just allow one voice within you to affect the way you think?

The Rare You

People will rarely see you the way that you see yourself, but don't let it stress you out. You most likely don't see people the way they see themselves either. We selectively choose what to see in others based on our purpose of having them in our lives. We may see others the way that they like to be seen, but not the way that they really are, because what we see is only a snapshot that is bound to a certain time, to a certain angle, and to a certain state of mind that we have. Everything is relative, and nothing about you that people see is a pure truth because no one is perfect, and no characteristic in you can ever be applicable a hundred percent of the time. The only truth that holds place is that you have a certain capacity to cause a change in others based on what you can or cannot offer them. This capacity depends on your willingness to act upon it. If you believe that you can inspire others to change their ways and see themselves for who they are, and you are willing to go ahead and do it, then you are brave. You are rare. If you choose to keep that capacity within you without sharing it with those who can benefit from it, then you are no different than most people who choose to remain neutral. Which one are you?

The First Step

In order to achieve greatness, you have to be willing to take the right steps toward it. Some of us will settle for what is average. Some of us will settle for what will get us by in life. But some of us do not accept anything less than what is extraordinary, and this is where the most stress is bound to come our way. What stands between us and that extraordinary goal are hundreds of steps, and that blocks our image of that end goal. When we can't see it, we start losing hope, and we start losing belief that we are headed in the right direction. We could stand in front of the first step for as long as we want and waste time. Or we could go ahead and take the first step. Once we do that, it's hard not to go to the next step, and the next, because we don't want to lose what we just invested. Instead of looking too far ahead to see that end goal, pay attention to how you can nail the next step and believe in your heart that your end goal exists. Now do you see why some things in life are better than others? Because they are rare, and rarely will people intend to achieve them because of the uncertainty of being able to reach them. So, if you have an extraordinary goal, go for it. Take the first step. Giving up is not easy, but holding on is definitely harder. Once you can convince yourself of that and bring yourself to accept that you need to expect hardships in pursuit of greatness, then you have taken your first step graciously. You wouldn't worry about reaching for the fruits on the highest branches of a tree before planting the seed, would you?

A Moment In Between

Between all the rain and shadows, the clouds and darkness, the nights and their troubles, there are moments of sunshine that you must learn to cherish. Just like sadness doesn't last too long, those moments of happiness might not either. Put happiness in your heart when it comes your way as you would put sadness. You are not being selfish by doing that. You deserve to be happy. And moments of happiness come just like moments of sadness. Moments of sunshine come just like moments of rain. You can choose to bask in the sun, just as you choose to get drenched in the rain.

A Serene State of Mind

If you're not at peace with your thoughts, don't expect anyone to express theirs to you. If you're not at peace with your feelings, don't expect anyone to be honest with you about theirs. If you can't be at peace with the closest people to you, don't expect new people to enter your life. If you're not at peace with your past, don't expect a hopeful future to come easily. Peace starts from within. It reflects on your outside whether you are aware of it or not. It is the beauty of your soul that reflects the purity from within you. Be at peace with yourself so that you may be content and happy with being who you are, or else you will be living in conflict with no one other than yourself, and you will become in need of help from someone who is not you. Don't depend on anyone to answer your questions. Don't depend on anyone to give you clarity. Find the answers yourself. Find clarity yourself. You have a brain to guide you and a heart to motivate you.

Take That Step

If you can't stand up for what you believe in, prepare to be silenced. If you don't have the courage to pursue your dreams, prepare for someone else reaching them. If you don't have the strength to hold on to what really matters in your life, then prepare for it to let go of you. If you can't take the initiative to take the step forward that will give you a better future, then prepare for that future to step further away from you. Quit blaming your surroundings for the consequences that you cause for yourself. Lead your life and follow your dreams, not people.

Beyond What Your Eyes See

Do you ever wonder what's hidden in people's hearts? About what makes them who they are? About their values and beliefs? About the battles they fought? The battles they won and lost? The ones they are still fighting? Do you ever wonder what's behind every brave smile? Or do you just look at the outer appearance of a person and assume that you know what you need to know? The reality is that we often forget that each person has a history that made them who they are. We forget that the snapshot we're getting of a person's life is one that could not possibly be enough to represent that history or give them credit for it. Why do we do that? Is it because it's just easier to judge a book by its cover? Is it more convenient? And, does that mean that we should look at ourselves that way too? Just worry about polishing up our outsides and not worry about bettering our inner selves? This is a serious problem that we face. We think that way because it's easier to care for how people perceive us than to care about who we really are on the inside and how we perceive ourselves. We condense our whole being and our whole worth into how we look on the outside. Don't ever think that a second you take to reflect and think about your own life is selfish. Make who you are into who you want to be. Don't let who you are make you who you don't want to be.

Dream

No dream is ever too big, and no step toward a dream is ever too small. Believe that you will get there, and you will. Your doubts will only hold you back and make each step harder, each decision harder, and each change harder. Celebrate the little successes so that you may appreciate the bigger ones. Learn from the little failures so that you may learn how to deal with the bigger ones. Be at peace with yourself, for you cannot achieve peace with the world if you can't be at peace with yourself. Give more than you take and don't give anything because you expect to get something in return. Be genuine. Truly wish goodness from your heart. The world will have no other option but to smile back at you and grant you the happiness that you define for yourself. What does happiness mean to you?

Write Your Happiness

What makes your life unique? Life is full of ups and downs. It is full of good moments and bad moments, amazing times and times when you are desperate for anything good to happen. If life came with a manual, it would be full of blank pages that you would fill out yourself. There would be pages that you wish you could rip out but can't, pages that you wish you could stay on and not turn, pages that you would love to erase and rewrite. Those wishes and those feelings are what make your life unique, irreplaceable. There is no one path to happiness, no one path to uniqueness. There is no one path to success. So, instead of wasting your time looking for prescribed steps to take to make your life perfect, pave your own steps. Create your own landmarks. Walk your own path. You will not feel the greatness of your success unless you make it unique to yourself, unless you direct your strengths in the right direction and use your weaknesses to your advantage. Avoid the defined black-and-white rules set by others. Be genuine with whatever you do. Make your own colors and shine.

Figuring You Out

If time did not exist, would patience exist? If hearts did not exist, would love exist? If minds did not exist, would logic exist? If hardships did not exist, would perseverance exist? Would the night exist if we had no day to look forward to? And would opportunity exist if we had no motivation to reach for it? Would dreams exist if there were no dreamers? Would a bright today exist without a hopeful yesterday? Everything you have in your life is present because of the existence of something else. If you ever have a problem with one aspect, look for what it is associated with. Maybe then your eyes will see the root of the problem. For example, if you have a problem with patience, maybe you need to manage your time or use it more wisely to take your mind off of what makes you impatient. Don't isolate your problems. Don't take them out of the context that they were created in. No problem is created without the solution preexisting, and figuring out that solution is up to no one but you.

Moments to Live For

Think back to the moments when you felt that you'd made a difference in someone's life. Think back to the moments when you saw someone else's eyes light up because they saw the best in themselves through your eyes. Think back to the moments when your efforts to make someone realize what they are capable of doing finally started having an impact on them. Think back to the times when you felt that you were standing at the edge of a cliff, uncertain whether jumping would take you down to the lowest valley of disappointment or fly you up to the highest sky of happiness. Think back to the moments when happiness came so fast at you that you lost track of time, of space, of logic. Think back to the moments when you did something good for the sake of goodness without anyone knowing but yourself. Think back to the moments when you chose silence over words because words could not do justice to your thoughts, whether it was a happy or sad silence. Think back to the moments when your smile could not possibly contain your happiness, when your heart ceased to beat so fast. Think back to those moments, and tell me, isn't your life truly worth living? Weren't those moments truly critical for making you who you are? Be thankful for those moments so that you don't become immune to them when they happen again and again, because they most definitely will. Whether you notice them or not is based on how much you've cherished them before.

What Would You Do?

Often the moments that take our breath away are those unplanned, those that we have long hoped for but, deep down, feel hopeless about. Those moments seem as far away as the stars, and as admirable and desirable as light is to a butterfly. What is the one thing that's been constantly on your mind lately? Think about it and think of how much energy you're putting into thinking about it, into the *what if this* and *but what if that*, into what you would do if it happened or what you would do if it didn't happen, into what your next step would be, into thinking of ways to stop thinking about it if you didn't get it. Think. Now imagine that what you have been thinking about was given to you at the time when you least expected it, when you really were putting every effort into looking away from it. At a time when all you wanted to do was ignore its existence in your head because you'd thought about it for way too long and figured that it just was not giving you any sign of being the right thing for you. Imagine that it was given to you in a place where you least expected to get what you wanted, because it was a strange place, a beautiful place that made you wonder about how great life could be if you could rid yourself of that nagging thought. Would it make you hopeful again? Would it make that thought come back even stronger? Would it make you happy? Or would it make you want to walk away even faster because you finally got what you wanted after realizing that you could live happily without it?

In Case You've Ever Wondered

Sometimes I wonder if my dreams are too big for the world, or if the world is too small for my dreams. Somehow, life always pushes me in the direction of following my dreams. Being hopeful has never left me hopeless. Being thankful has never left me unthankful. Being happy has honestly never left me sad. Being compassionate has never left me heartless, and being grateful has never left me ungrateful. Being honest with myself has never left me feeling guilty or insincere. Living up to my own expectations can be difficult because my expectations for myself are too high. But are they better than others' expectations for me? Definitely. Are they more relevant to my life and my dreams than others' expectations for me? Absolutely! So, today I encourage you to be hopeful, thankful, happy, compassionate, grateful, and honest with yourself. Start off with positive outlooks because they will never end up negatively, regardless of what those around you may tell you. Ignore negative advice. Follow your dreams. Live up to your expectations. And remember, it's okay to be hard on yourself sometimes because no one knows what you are capable of doing more than yourself. Don't fall short of the greatness you know is in you. Believe in yourself. Trust your judgments and set out for your dreams. They may be closer than you think.

Take It or Leave It

Be the one to always give and not expect anything in return. Give, not to avoid being hurt but to feel content with what you can do yourself, to be independent, to be happy without needing anyone to give you happiness. Be like a breeze of change that inspires others to see their abilities without needing you to stay. Make people think. Make them wonder, and let them know that what you give is only based on what they are willing to take. Don't attribute your success based on whether you make a difference with everyone you meet but on the kind of difference you are willing to make. Accept that you have no ownership over people even if you do give them more than you receive. The effort that you put into inspiring others to value their own selves, and to see the best in themselves, gives them two choices: either to take it or leave it. Whatever they choose is not a sign of your success or failure unless you believe that to be the case.

Educate Me

Educate me, not by making me memorize facts but by teaching me how to read between the lines, how to critically think, how to deeply understand. Educate me by respecting me. Educate me by treating me as a human. Educate me by showing me that you make mistakes just like I do. Educate me by showing me that I am not perfect, and neither are you. As long as I can teach myself to get back up, it's okay if I fall down. Educate me by telling me where to look, but not what to see. Educate me by respecting yourself so that I may respect you, so that I may respect myself. Educate me by seeing the best in me because, while you might not know it, you may be my only hope. Educate me by believing in me. Make me believe that no question is ever stupid and no dream is ever too big. Educate me by making me love to learn. Educate me by taking away the fear of tests, marks, and standardization. Where I start and where I end are not as important as the journey I had to take from one to the other. Educate me by making me more dependent on myself and less dependent on you. Educate me by making me want to learn on my own. Educate me by making education about me, about making me a lifelong learner, by making me able to teach myself. Educate me by making me think of the world, not just words and pictures in a textbook. Educate me by empowering me, by making me truly believe that I can make a difference in the world, because while I am unique, I am not living alone. Educate me by telling me the sky is my limit. Put me at the intersection and equip me with the skills, not only the knowledge, to choose which path to take.

Human Me

When I claim to be perfect, you can claim that I'm a hypocrite. When I claim to make no mistakes, you can claim that I'm egocentric. When I claim that I'm always good at what I do, you can claim that I'm arrogant. I am not perfect. I am not flawless. I am not the best at everything I do. I have imperfections. I have flaws. I make mistakes. But I'll tell you one thing that I am. I am respectful. I listen to you when you speak. I help you whenever I can. I appreciate you, and I see the best in you. I see the good in you before I see the bad. I always have a chance to give you. I respect you as a human and hope that you will do the same for your own sake.

Read My Silence

If you think my silence has no meaning, think twice. Think, and you will realize the strength I hold back my words with. The most universal language is that of silence. We all use it, but it is the most misunderstood. It is the most powerful. It is the only language that we all express yet each have our own unique way of expressing. Go for those who understand your own silence no matter what you coat it with. Go for those who are aware of the existence of a meaning behind your silence, one that is deeper than what any words can rightfully express. After all, if they don't understand your silence, they will never understand your words.

I Deserve It

I'd rather be disappointed by the truth than satisfied with a lie. Respect me, not because I respect you but because I deserve your respect. How pleased would you be if you found out I respected you only because I wanted you to respect me back or because I wanted something in return? I respect you because you deserve it. Don't listen to me just because I listen to you. I listen to you because you deserve to be heard. Don't be nice to me just because I'm nice to you. I'm nice to you because you deserve to be treated right. Don't show me that you care just because you know I care. I care for you because your heart needs care. If your thoughts and feelings are not genuine, point them in a direction other than mine. If I only give you what you deserve, at least keep me away from what I don't deserve.

Never Doubt

You may doubt that the moonlight will always enlighten your way
in the darkest of nights. You may doubt that the sun will always
strike its rays through the gloomiest of clouds to brighten your days.
You may doubt that a rainbow will come after every storm, or that
a shining star of hope will always be there for you to wish upon.
But never doubt that there are people out there who will be your
light in the darkest of nights, who will brighten your every day, and
who will open your eyes to the bright side of every situation. Never
doubt that there are people out there whose wishes are not for things
of their own but whose wishes are to make your wishes come true.
Give your soul a chance at being happy by truly believing that those
people exist. If you exist, then they do.

Perspective

The direction that you're looking in may be great, not because of itself but because of what it's making you look away from.

When You Lose Hope

Don't allow a few humans who shattered your belief in humanity make you believe that good humans don't exist. They do exist. And the biggest proof is that you exist. If you exist in this world, you'd better believe that there are people like you out there. So when you find them, be their friend, empower them, give them a voice, give them the care and love and kindness that you would give to everybody else out there in the world. But because you know how much you need it, being the good heart that you are, give it to them in abundance.

Open Your Eyes

If they don't care when you care, they won't care when you don't.
So stop trying to show that you care or that you don't. Either way,
you're at a loss because the efforts you're putting into showing that
you care are going toward the wrong people. Direct them toward
those who care when you care and care when you don't care. While
you're trying to prove a point, you may be blind to those who care
for you. Not every person who has eyes can see everything. We do
select what we want to see and make ourselves blind to what we
don't. Ask yourself if what you're looking at is worth it. Open your
eyes to new things that may have been there for a while, waiting for
you to look back.

I Wonder

Before you wonder *why*, ask yourself how you got to that question. Ask yourself about what you did to reach that *why*. Often, the answer to it lies in what you did to get to it. Don't open a door and wonder why it opened. Don't open a door unless you are able to close it. Don't walk down a path and wonder why you got to a certain destination. Don't walk down a path without knowing your way back. That doesn't mean you can't take risks. That doesn't mean you shouldn't reflect. But don't take a risk and wonder why you failed, separating what you did from the outcome. You have to take responsibility for the decisions you make, for the things you do, and for the words you say. Then you will realize the presence of the answer to your *why* within the question itself. My destination was a product of the decisions I took to get to it, from the times I said *no* when I should have said *yes* and from the times I said *yes* when I should have said *no*.

Better Places

There will always be places that don't welcome you, people who don't want you in their lives, and dreams that just don't work out. But that doesn't mean that there aren't other places that will welcome you. That doesn't mean that there aren't other people who would love to have you in their lives. And that doesn't mean that there aren't bigger dreams for you. Maybe you're meant to be in better places. Maybe you're meant to have better people in your life. Maybe you are meant to reach higher dreams than the ones that you have planned. So don't despair, trust in fate, and go for what you truly believe is the best thing for you or that puts your heart and soul at peace. And it will work out.

The Power of Words

Your words can be more healing than any kind of medicine. They can be more toxic than any kind of poison. They can ease a mind of its nagging questions. They can relieve a heart from its doubts. They can free a heart from the chains that keep it holding on and that make it fear letting go. They can spring hope into a deserted heart. They can shatter a soul barely holding on to the pieces that make it strong. They can be a shelter for the broken and a canon of motivation for those who need confidence. They can build mountains of confidence and build stairs to those dreams that hide above the clouds. They can dig holes into the darkest and deepest of scars. They can strike happiness into the souls in most need of it, and they can strike sadness into the souls of those most far away from it. So, before you speak, ask yourself if your words are true. If they are not, then you are fooling the hopeless into hope that won't last. You are breaking down walls temporarily that will be built even higher afterward. Say what the truth and genuineness in your heart need to say. Say no more.

Never Settle

If you choose an option because it's the only one, then you haven't chosen. You've settled.

Seal My Lips

If you understand me, then you've enslaved part of me. So, if you don't take care of my words, I will protect the pieces of my soul through the silence of my lips.

Negative Intentions

If my strength intimidates you, I hope you realize that's a weakness of yours. If my strength doesn't impress you, I hope you never see my weaknesses because, if you can't be happy to see me at my best, you most likely will be happy to see me at my worst.

Together

Lucky you. I don't build walls. I build strong values that take me up higher. I work on my strength, my confidence, and my independence. So, do you need to work hard to get to me? Yes. Must you take the right steps to get up there? Definitely. You see, I don't want you to break down a wall I've built only to realize that I'm at the same level as everyone else you know. I also don't want you to climb a wall only to come down it on the other side. I want you to actually come up higher for yourself and for me so that we can both say that we've worked hard to build what we have, not worked hard to get to each other, because, once we do, what's next?

Wake Up to the Darkness

As long as I breathe, I learn. As long as I have a purpose, I live. As long as I have a goal, I progress. As long as I have something to live for, I fight. As long as I struggle, I hope. I am what I do, and who I am is not who you see. I am who you understand. Do you know why? Who I think you are is not who you really are either. Unless I try to understand you, I may never really know who you are. I may never see your inner beauty. We all wear the masks that we think make us more beautiful. We claim to love what deserves our love, but we end up loving what we can't have because it adds purpose and meaning to our lives. It gives us challenges that we need to work for and overcome. Even if what we deserve comes easily, we let it go. Sometimes we don't even notice it because sometimes, no matter how bright the light may be, we don't notice its existence until the darkness comes.

Sometimes

Sometimes you choose not to walk through an open door, not because it's not inviting but because a closed door makes you wonder, makes you anticipate, and makes you crave the challenge of opening it. A closed door makes you want to work hard. It makes you want to take the risk of knocking. This is when you realize the irony of your will to accept waiting in front of a closed door over having the guarantee of being able to walk through an open door. This is when you realize that sometimes, just sometimes, you need to close your door so others can knock on it. Sometimes you need to stop shining so others can notice your existence. Sometimes you need to stop answering unasked questions so others can start wondering.

Know Yourself

Don't aim to be understood by others before you understand yourself. People may never understand your intentions. You know them. They may never understand why you do what you do or say what you say. You know the reasons. They may never understand why you treat them the way that you do, or why you treat others the way that you do. You know why. They may never understand the words that you say or the language your eyes speak. You understand these languages because you create them. They may never understand the strength it takes to be the way that you are. You know your weaknesses and your struggles, and you are the one who works to overcome them, so your strength means more to you than it could ever mean to anyone else. It really isn't about what they understand by just looking at you. It's about what they want to understand, and if they really want to, they won't assume. They will ask.

The Other Side

You may think that I share my strengths with you to put you down and to tell you that I'm better. But have you ever thought that I had to overcome the fear of you envying my happiness, hoping that you could be happy not for me but with me? You may think that I share you my weaknesses only because I need you to help me cope with them, but have you ever thought that I had to overcome my safe silence to express my words to you? Have you ever thought that I've made the decision to allow you to understand me? You may think that I am nice to you because I need something from you, but have you ever thought that I had to silence every disappointment I've had in the past, and every unnoticed effort, to be nice to you? You may think that I care for the person that I want you to be, not who you really are, but have you ever thought that if I thought you were not worthy of my care that I would allow myself to care for you?

Close Your Door

The moments when you feel de-realized from life are critical moments to reflect on what is essential to your existence. If you don't put yourself first, no one will. Learn to stop when you've done just enough. In the same way that you say sorry when you don't have to, you need to hear it, at least, when you rightfully deserve it. You know the things and people that you promise yourself will make you happy if you push yourself hard enough to get them? They will make you happy for a while until your inner need for happiness asks for something new. Real happiness comes from within, from what you have now, not from what you will have tomorrow. Close your door. If something belongs in your life, it'll knock. You have enough things and people around you to make you happy. Don't just look at them. See them. Appreciate them. Say no when you need to, not only inside, but say it loudly enough to be heard. Extend your hand only for as long as you need to and only to the extent that doesn't hurt you. You know why? It's because, once you fall, it's not what you want that will lift you up but what you already have.

Unjustified Excuses

There's absolutely nothing wrong with giving people excuses. It just goes to show how positive you are deep down, how able you are to see the good in people, and how able you are to see past the faces that they show. The real mistake is when you treat those people as if they've tried to express those excuses to you, as if they've put the effort forward to clarify their words or actions. The problem is when you make those excuses into apologies in your own head and forgive without being asked forgiveness or even being thought of as worthy of being asked for forgiveness. The problem is when you don't allow people to feel the need to make an effort to hold a spot in your life. If you're going to keep making them feel that you're okay no matter what they do, then don't wonder why they continue to do what they do. If you're willing to spend hours trying to justify their actions, what have you left to worry about your own?

Past What You See

If only we knew the tests that each of us has encountered, we would be much more compassionate toward one another. But no. We see beauty, and we wonder why we don't have it. We see riches, and we wonder why we don't have them. We see happiness, and we wonder why we don't have it. We see contentment, commitment, and success, and we wonder why someone else has them. Little do you know that, while you're envying a person's beauty, money, or success, they may be battling to live. Those things that they have that you don't have may be a way of helping them cope. Those things may be a way of proving to them that perfection does not exist. It cannot exist. Just because people don't complain to you doesn't mean that they don't have problems. It means that they've learned to accept their problems and deal with them without wanting you to worry. They think of how to keep you happy while you wonder how they could be so happy. Don't judge. Don't give yourself the right to decide whether a person deserves what he or she has or doesn't have. If you were able to see through people's smiles and into their hearts, you would regret every judgment you wrongfully made. You would take back every wish you made, even between you and yourself, of harm happening to them. Worry about yourself. Appreciate what you have. Don't look past what you can't possibly understand. Be careful what you wish for. Life may give you something that you want but take away something that you need.

Lesson Learned

Sometimes we get so stuck on fixing things that we forget that it could be more worth it to throw them out. And sometimes it's not the things that are broken but the way we think of them, because of the past they remind us of or the fact that we think of them in the first place. That's why it's good to have people in your life who will tell you when you're wrong or when you need to stop thinking. Not people who will tell you what you want to hear but people who will tell you what you need to hear so that you may truly be a better person and perceive reality the way it is, not the way you think it is.

Take Care

Some people deserve your eyes if they need them, and some people don't deserve a look from your eyes. But, life isn't about what people deserve or don't deserve. Life is not fair. Be honest with yourself. Half the time you probably don't give yourself what you deserve. You allow your heart to love before your mind can tell you, *Stop. You deserve more.* You allow yourself to extend your hand before your mind can tell you, *Be careful whose hand you're holding.* You say *yes* knowing that soon you will wish you said *no.* You walk down a path without knowing that you can come back. You even believe in others more than you believe in yourself sometimes. You believe in others' ability to make you feel better more than in your own ability to do so. So, before you expect others to be fair with you, be fair to yourself. Before you get disappointed that people didn't give you what you think you deserve, give yourself what you deserve. Those who tell you that it's a rich man's world know what they're talking about. It's not about the money but the degree to which you think of yourself. Don't confuse taking care of yourself, your self-worth, and self-esteem with selfishness, egocentrism, or being stuck up. It's not black or white. Create the shade of balance between the care that you give and that which you receive that is perfect for you.

That Path

The breaks you create on the inside can break you down more than those on the outside. Any stranger on the street will help you get back up when you fall and hurt yourself, but rarely will you find someone who will see the agony in your eyes and work to replace it with a smile. You claim to be the one to see the sadness in others' eyes, while it is you who creates the sadness in their eyes to give yourself the excuse to make them happy. Because you want to make them happy. Because you tie your happiness to theirs. And those who actually care about you, you ignore, gracefully, telling yourself that they don't need you. Because you don't need them. Because you couldn't tie your happiness to theirs.

Accept Yourself

Don't look for acceptance. Look for respect. If you get it, give it back, and if you don't, be the first to give it. If you don't get it back, keep moving forward. If you kill yourself over every person who doesn't treat you the same way that you treat them, you'll waste your time worrying about changing people who don't care about changing themselves in the first place. If you make yourself believe that you need people to accept you, then you are giving them the right to reject you. You don't need anyone to accept you. You need to accept yourself. You need to respect yourself. You can't make anyone understand you. You can't make anyone listen to you. You can't make anyone love you, trust you, or even like you. In the same way that you decide to make them important to you, give them the right to make that decision too. If they don't, it's not your responsibility to change the way they think of you. It's your responsibility to change the way you think of yourself. Before you expect people to put themselves in your shoes, put yourself in your own shoes. Worry about changing what you need to change.

It's You

You have to realize the difference between people who consistently disrespect you because of the way you deal with them and those who disrespect you because of who you are. Often, you blame yourself for the way that people treat you. Let me tell you, you're right to believe that it's something that has to do with you. You know why? It's because they just might be jealous of who you are. So give yourself a pat on the back for being good enough to make people envy a quality in you. They won't admit it. In fact, they will claim to praise you for it, but deep down they may be burning to see you lose it. They will push you to the limit to make you just like them. What a world we have to live in where living *happily* and *peacefully* means being silent, following without questioning, and living without dreaming. Don't ever allow anyone to make you feel that being a good person is something bad. Don't ever allow anyone to make you feel that you need to prove anything to them. You don't have to prove anything to anyone if you've got the proof you need for yourself. Believe in yourself. Believe in goodness. Live your life the way you know you want to. Think of yourself, but don't be selfish. Seek wealth of knowledge and spirit, not wealth of money. Love and allow people to love you. Give more than you take. Take, but don't be greedy. Respect people, but don't allow them to walk all over you. Speak, but only when you need to. Choose silence unless it's going to hurt you. It's better for your words to hurt others than for your silence to hurt you. But trust me, you don't need to have people in your life who will make you choose between those two options.

The Little Things

Give yourself time to evaluate what happens around you. Don't read into everything. Learn to dissociate from the past and focus on the present. See the positives. Learn to believe that what others do or say cannot affect you unless you allow it to. So, although your tired little heart might hurt despite how strong it wants to be, despite how strong it knows that it can be, you need to protect it.

Your Opinion of Me

Sometimes it hurts more to stay away from what hurts you than to keep allowing it to hurt you. That's why you make excuses when they don't exist. That's why you create hope that, ironically, makes you hopeless. That's why you put locks on doors before you try to open them. Life is simple. Love is everywhere. You just have to change where you're looking. You have to change what you're seeing. See the best in yourself before you see it in others because, if you can't see the best in yourself, you will come to believe the worst that people believe of you. You will fool yourself into believing that their opinion of you is essential to your happiness. Be honest with yourself for a moment. Those who see the impact that they have on your life and choose to use it in a manipulative way do not belong in your life. A true leader will tell you to stop following him if he notices that you're following. A manipulative person will be happy to see your willingness to do whatever is asked of you. I'm not saying that you need to remove these people from your life. I'm just telling you to stop associating your happiness with theirs if they don't consider you a part of it. Stop equating your worth with their opinion of you.

No Time to Waste

Life's too short, and it's so easy to convince yourself that you need to just worry about working as much as you can, making as much as you can, while you can. Come to think about it, there has got to be more to life than this. What's your purpose from all of it? At the end of your life, what do you want to look back and see that you've accomplished? What did you invest your time in? What things and people did you put first? What and whom did you neglect? Some things are more important than others, and to be honest, we often neglect those who love us the most. Most times, this is not intentional but is because their love is so great for us that it makes us feel so safe. So safe, in fact, that we feel we will never lose it, that we will never lose them, that they will always understand. Those people did not have to love us, but they chose to love us. Those people chose us over sleep when they needed it most, chose us over money when they could have made more of it. Those people are your parents. They brought you into this world, and all of a sudden, you became their world. You filled up a space that they didn't know they had. You helped them discover a kind of love they didn't know existed. You always had to worry about yourself, but they had to worry about you and them too. Don't wait until it's too late to show them your love and gratitude.

The Gift of Gentleness

Not everyone you meet will give you the respect or love that you deserve. Respect them anyway. Love them anyway. No matter what you do, be kind. It is better to be kind and be hurt than to be unkind and cause pain. You were given the gift of gentleness and kindness. You were given the gift of a soft heart. So do not lose it. Do not allow your heart to harden. Just because someone caused you pain, it does not mean that everyone will. Just because someone betrayed your trust, it does not mean that others aren't trustworthy. Just because someone broke your heart, it does not mean that it will remain broken forever. It is better to love with a whole heart, to give with a whole heart, and to trust with a whole heart than to never experience the beauty of love, the reward of giving, and the comfort of trusting. And when you fall hard, you can choose to remain on the ground for as long as you want, but you can also choose to get back up. Love again. Give again. Trust again. It is the experience that grows you, not the fear of it.

Choose Happiness

The happiness that your dreams promise you may be right around the corner, but you can reach them only if you're willing to turn the corner. Walk away from your safe place of hopeless uncertainty. Unchain your heart from the uncertainty that's been grounding it to misery. Choose happiness and walk away.

Imagine

The reality you live in is partially up to you. The fantasy you live in is entirely up to you.

Pure

I've learned to assume good intentions before bad ones, not because I'm naive but because I'd rather assume good and be wrong than assume bad and be wrong.

Respect Me

If you must explain to others why they need to respect you, they better wonder why you respect them in the first place. If they don't think you deserve to be treated with the most basic human value, what makes them think they deserve it?

Take Care of You

I had an interesting conversation with a wise, old stranger the other day, and she inspired this thought. Take care of yourself for yourself. If you do it for others, you will start to equate your self-worth with theirs. You'll start to equate your happiness with theirs. You'll start seeing yourself through their eyes, and all their eyes can see is what you look like on the outside. They can but don't see your heart, but you can feel your heart. Yet you choose not to acknowledge it. You start to wonder whether they could ever see themselves through your eyes. You'll be disappointed to realize that you were not able to feel that you deserved to be happy because of the uniqueness within you because you chose to tie your happiness to those who couldn't tie their happiness to yours.

A Fateful Sky

Never give up on the happiness that your heart deserves. Believe in fate. Believe in its power to lead you to the places where you belong. Believe in its power to make you miss the places you've never been, love the people you haven't met, and cherish the memories you haven't lived yet. You know where you were born, but do you know where your soul will rise from? People oceans away are united by the sky, by the stars that have been wished upon over and over again. Even the moon disappears on us sometimes, but we know it's there. We know it's coming back. We just have to be patient. All we have to do is wait, for the perfect moment is not the one that you plan but the one that happens despite what you have planned.

The Stars Within

I've gotten used to telling my secrets to the stars because they understand the language of my heart and mind like no one else does. They never ask questions. They always listen. I believe in them, just as they believe in me. Their beauty never discourages me from dreaming. After all, if I can trust something that distant from me, how can I not trust that I will reach the dreams that may seem too far out of reach? So I started thinking. Why did I choose the stars? Why did I not choose something closer, someone closer? After much thought, I realized that the stars were just an excuse that I used for communication with myself. I taught myself to listen to my own heart and to not make others listen to it before myself. I taught myself to listen to my mind before speaking its deepest thoughts to those around me. I taught myself to understand myself, to coach myself, to motivate myself. I taught myself to be honest with myself before I am honest with anyone else, or else my honesty with others will be a deception to my own self, because who could possibly be more worthy of the truth than myself? I taught myself to respect myself, to respect my path, to respect the freedom I was given the moment I took my first breath on this earth. I made the stars wonder about me just as much as I've wondered about them. I taught myself to see the best in myself, to believe in myself, and to not allow anyone to make me doubt myself. I allowed myself to see happiness in the simplest of things because I truly believe that if I can't see the beauty of the stars, I may never appreciate the beauty of a full moon.

Smile

Never doubt that your smile may lighten up someone's day without you even knowing it. So smile often. Frown less. See happiness in the simplest of things. Express gratitude more often, and you will be just like a ray of sunshine over the darkest of hearts and, most importantly, over the hearts of those who matter to you.

Reframe Gratitude

We always complain that we are given more than what we can handle. It's true. If we only knew what that truly meant, we would stop complaining and start showing more gratitude. Take a moment to be honest with yourself and think deeply. Reflect. Think of all of the things that you have. Are you handling them correctly? You are given a heart that has the capacity to love until no limit can be drawn, but, somehow, you build a tiny little wall around it to *protect* it. But what are you protecting it from? What keeps it beating? Your heart has the capacity to give because it wants to, not because it has to, but somehow you convince yourself to stop it from giving unless it must. It has the capacity to flutter with happiness over the simplest, most beautiful details of life: a child's smile, a mother's hug, a random act of kindness on the street, the determination in someone's eyes, a kind word, etc. Yet, somehow, you make it immune to seeing those things because you're so busy looking for bigger sources of happiness, not realizing that if you can't appreciate the little things, you can never appreciate the bigger ones. They may satisfy you temporarily, but they will never bring you true happiness simply because they don't last, or your interest in them fades. You have a mind that has the capacity to be the most logical. It can talk you through any kind of problems that you have, yet you convince yourself that others can solve them for you better than you can. Your mind has the ability to put you first, yet you allow yourself to let others make you doubt yourself. Before you complain of being given more than what you can handle, think of everything that you already have that you take for granted. If you think that you've been given more than what you can handle, you must have been given more than what you deserve.

People Who Are Good for You

There are people who notice you only when you shine, or when you fall into the darkness. Not the average you. Not the mediocre you. But the great you, or the not-so-great you. The people who are worthiest of your care are not those who only notice you at your best and worst but those who see you at all times. They don't need an excuse to love you. They don't need an excuse to talk to you, or to ask you how you're doing. They don't need an excuse to share their happiness with you. They don't need an explanation. They give you one without you asking for it. They assume the good in you before the bad. So keep eyes open just so you don't miss those people. Once you find them, never let them go because those are not just friends but family members. They're life companions. They are the people who will tell you when you are wrong simply because they've allowed themselves to tie their well-being to yours.

Soul Food

Nurture your heart with the love of those who love you regardless of how hard it is to want what you already have. Contentment is bliss, and happiness flies on the wings of gratitude. Love them back. Give to them without expecting them to give to you equally in return. True care cannot handle expectations of balance at all times because not every person needs the same thing at the same time. Sometimes we must love more than we feel the love back. We must care more than we feel the care back. Because that gives us the gratification that we need to feel that we've made the difference that we can make for a person who was in need of it. Remember that every strength becomes stronger by weakening the weakness that it spurs from. Every success becomes more victorious by weakening the sense of pride that comes with it. Every happiness becomes more rewarding by weakening the sense of selfishness associated with it. So, today, try to be strong by overcoming the fears you have because you created those fears, as no one can get rid of them but you. Be successful by seeing yourself as the winner because your goal is to learn, not to win. Be happy by giving happiness to others.

Moonless Nights

Even on moonless nights, the stars don't cease to shine. Even when the clouds conceal the sun in weary skies, every creature believes in its existence. Even when the thirsty bits of earth long for the slightest mist of water, they always accept the rain, no matter how long it takes. The branches of abandoned trees never reject to give rest to a restless bird. Even death springs new life in our hearts as it awakens our sleepless souls to the beauty of the life that we have and were complaining about. So tell me this. How can you be great if you expect to take more than you give? How can you expect to be different if you settle for being the same as everyone else? How can you lose hope after failing once? How can you tell your heart not to accept love after it's been hurt? Or your mind to cease to believe or trust after it's been deceived? How can you be afraid not to meet your fate at the right time, when fate is what chases you, not what you chase? The life you have ahead of you is a journey, and happiness is not a destination. Faith is in the heart, but it plants its seeds in your actions. If you work by your principles, you'll never make a decision that you'll later regret. No matter what fate it is you're chasing that you think is yours, none but what is meant for you will happen. Believe. Let the uniqueness of your heart overflow with hopeful patience that the happiness it deserves already exists and that, because of your uniqueness, it will come in a unique way.

Just a Moment

The moment you use to take care of yourself lessens your need for the care of others to feel better about yourself. Take care of yourself. Take care of your heart. Take care of your mind. And they will take care of you.

A New Look

If I judge you based on your past, I'd be creating for myself a past that one day I'll be judged for. Don't weave imaginary jail bars around people because of what they've done. At least they have experience. At least they've learned. What do you have? What have you learned? Give people new chances. Allow them to see a pure world through your eyes. Be the source of their belief in goodness still existing. Look at who they have become and who they want to be. Welcome people into your life with faith in their goodness and in their potential. You're in need of that just as much as they are.

Grow Stronger

Just as a fire gives rise to new, stronger growth in a forest, every time you burn out, you have a chance to grow even stronger. Just remember to reflect. Know where you are before you try to figure out where you want to be. If you don't know where you're leaving from, you can't possibly know what you need to do to get to your destination. Stay strong. Pave your own way with every effort you put forth. That's truly when you feel authentic accomplishment. Along the way, don't forget to be grateful for it all, both the good and the bad.

A Little Wiser

With every year of your life, you will realize the following. You will know more people, but less people will know you. More people may exist in your life. Many people may know of you, but very few will really know you. Most people exist in your life to know what you're up to, rather than really care for you. You will be the friend of more people, but you will have fewer friends. But your friends will be like mirrors of your soul because, by speaking to them, you are speaking to yourself. You will speak less and listen more. Way more. You will keep more secrets than the secrets you give. You will be more tolerant but less tolerated. You may own more things, but less things will own you. You will be the master of your emotions, and only you will be able to expose them. The older you get, the more of your childhood innocence you'll appreciate and retrieve, because children think of the result before they think of the consequences. Before they jump, they think of where they'll land and not of the wounds the fall will cause. You will realize that you are unique in your thoughts because, most times, you will feel misunderstood. Because you refused to allow the world to mold you, you will always struggle to stay true to yourself in a world of people striving to meet the ideals that society has created. A one-size-fits-all that you refused to live up to.

All About You

Once you realize that half of your problems are caused by the way you think about things that come your way, and that the other half is caused by the way you deal with others' struggle to think of theirs, you will become at peace with yourself. You will be able to realize when you have the right to be angry and when you overreacted. You will realize when you have the right to take a stand and when you need to apologize. You will realize when you were selfish and when you were naive. You will be more aware of your purpose behind anything, and you will be able to tell yourself *stop* when you need to. Life is not all about your comfort; it is about mutual well-being while ensuring that you're as comfortable as you can be while being considerate about others' comfort. You will stay humble, although others' actions may make you feel superior. You will be a leader, not by the number of people who follow you but by the number of people whose lives you impact.

Love

I've never been in love, but I imagine it to be hard work. It is wanting for another person more than you want for yourself. It is giving without expecting the same in return. Once that expectation exists, problems are inevitable. It is having lots of arguments but never disrespect. Never humiliation, or even belittling. It's having someone who knows your weaknesses but who doesn't use them against you. Love is a sacred thing. It is by no means perfect, nor is it flawless. It is beautiful with every little imperfection in it. Perfection is always the same, but every imperfection makes each love a unique thing. Love is not a destination that we reach at one point. It is a journey that we already began the moment we were born. It is not something that you find but something you discover as you look more and more into your soul and learn more about yourself. It is having someone who makes you see the world in a better way. Someone who shifts your focus from the insignificant worries to the things that matter. Love never brings you down. It always lifts you up. It only grows. It is appreciating someone for who they are, not just for the way they make you feel. Love is seeing the beauty from within, for it is what lasts a lifetime. It is dedication to keep holding the hand of the one who loves you, even at heart. It is commitment to bettering oneself through the bettering of the other.

Goodness Is a Choice

Stopping yourself from doing what's wrong is not the same as choosing what's right and doing it. Don't stand on the verge of being good. Be as good as you can be. If you can give, give. If you can help, help. If you can make someone's day by a simple act of kindness, make it. Set the bar of success for yourself as high as the best that you can be, not as low as avoiding the worst that you can be. Big difference.

Take a Step Back

A sincere lack of effort is much more respectable than an insincere effort. If you sense insincerity, take a step back. If they think you're worth it, they'll take a step forward.

Say Something

Wake a wise man up about his oppression, and he will thank you for it. Wake a fool up about his oppression, and he will blame you for it. Yes, we all want to live peacefully and make our living without thinking of the bigger issues of power because that is just too big of a headache. We don't need to take responsibility for what we can't do anything about. Those who speak up get burned, and those who keep quiet are preferred. It's better to stay on the safe side, right? Wrong. You can always grow new skin when you burn, but you can't erase the propagation of oppression after you've allowed it. We are all born with conscious minds, so being oblivious to even the slightest form of oppression is a choice, not a result of unawareness. Be wise and stay awake. Just because you're breathing doesn't mean you're living. Do something. Say something. Risk something. At least, if you want to make a difference.

Unconditional Love?

Unconditional love is not true love. It's foolish love. True love has an unconditional willingness to listen and to understand. True love has an unconditional willingness to give, compromise, and sacrifice while working for one future, not two. It has conditions of respect. Don't tell me disrespect can come out of love. Don't tell me violence can come out of love. Don't tell me manipulation can come out of love. True love is not blind. It has a vision. Though it may not make sense who you love, how you love them should.

Work Hard

Thirty years from now, what do you want to look back and tell yourself? If you keep in mind the purpose you have in your life, every hard day becomes worth it. So, if you're working hard, work harder. Don't give up. Don't ever stop. Building yourself, though it is exhausting, is more rewarding than the regret of not doing so, especially when you realize that you're not as strong as you once were, or as capable as you once were.

How Dare You

If you have a purpose in life, you will have enemies. If you care about the well-being of the people around you, even if you don't know them, you will have enemies. The world will try to convince you that the best life that you can live is one in which you care about yourself only. Lose your heart. Don't be compassionate unless you have time. As long as you earn enough money, shut your mouth. Who cares about everyone else? Never question authority because doing that is wrong. Who are you to know more than those who are in positions of power? How dare you? We seriously have forgotten what being human means. We've become machines. We've become experts at justifying our flaws, but we're not even close to acknowledging that those flaws exist because of the lack of basic human interaction. How can a mother sacrifice years of her life, put her career aside, make her dreams wait, without waiting for a paycheck at the end of the month? Would a paycheck bring her the same kind of happiness anyway? Not. Even. Close. We don't make ourselves compassionate; we are born compassionate. We selectively allow ourselves to be heartless because we are convinced that selfish people who put themselves first are the happiest. Yes, put yourself first, but not in a selfish way. Put yourself first by working on bettering yourself. Listen to your heart when it tells you to help. Listen to it when it aches. Use your mind. Listen to it when it wakes up your dignity. Listen to it when it tells you to say no to what is wrong.

Your Inner Beauty

In an upside-down world like ours, it doesn't matter who you are. Who you make yourself seem like does, though. The higher your expectations, the harder people will work to reach them. And with your prestige, they value you more. It's true. But why do you look at materialistic people? Why do you look at those who make you feel like you have to be different to impress them? Stop and rewind. Go back to the caterpillar that you were before you got your beautiful wings. Who loved you then? Who respected you then? Who saw the beauty within you then? Those people right there are the ones who deserve to be impressed by you. Not the ones who make you feel small even though you're way bigger. Not the ones who make you feel worthless even though you deserve to be sitting on a throne in a kingdom of your own.

Heal

Don't point out people's mistakes unless you're willing to tell them how to fix them. Criticism can break the strongest of souls, and advice can build the weakest of spirits. Your words can be healing, or they can be sickening. Let them heal. Let them inspire. Let them be the crying shoulder that your shoulder cannot be.

Dusty Bookshelf

Some people are like good books. You would rather leave them on the shelf until you get the chance to give them your complete focus and undivided attention than read a page here and there. You want to understand every word, every line, and every message between the lines. The thing is, books can't move, but people can. If you wait too long before you pick them up, the dust on their hearts will have exhausted them and pushed them to leave.

Excuses

Do you ever find yourself restless, wondering whether giving them excuses means that you are weak and needy, or strong for holding on through the hard times? Do you find yourself feeling fed up with someone's inability to understand how small they make you feel when they continue to do what they know bothers you? You're torn between continuing to be patient and silent about it, and breaking your heart open in front of them to make them feel the depth of your hurt. Stop for a moment before you break just so your voice could be heard. Listen. The one who wants to hear you will hear you even in your deepest silence. The one who wants to understand you will dig the pain out of you and kiss it goodbye. Don't wait for someone to respect the value of your voice. Don't wait for someone whose existence in your life thrives on the excuses that you make for them. You deserve someone who will feel your pain when you're in pain, not someone who causes you pain on top of your pain.

Unspoken Words

When those who occupy a space in our hearts choose to treat us with silence, we fall. We crumble. We become paralyzed by their unspoken words. The words that chain us. The ones that stop us from being able to focus on anything that we have to do. They interrupt our thoughts and dwell there as unwelcomed visitors. They take the place of our thoughts and become the owners of our homes. Your home. My home. The owners of our minds. Your mind. My mind. Why do you let them own you? Tell me. If they are not your words, why do you let them own you? Does the sky own the sun just because the sun's rays strike through it?

Invisible

When the only eyes that you see yourself through do not see you, you quickly feel unseen. You feel invisible, with your presence being so heavy. You feel as if your mere existence is a burden. You struggle to feel the purpose in your presence. After all, what use is it to have all that you have if the one person whose eyes and heart you want to be seen by is blind to your own existence? Right? Wrong. Feeling hurt that the ones you care about don't see you is okay. But feeling useless and purposeless because of that is not okay. Your purpose and your worth do not depend on what they see. Waves in the middle of the ocean rage at night and during the day. Do they ask to be seen? Do they care if they are seen? They are part of the ocean and they own their right to exist within it just by being. Just because they don't see you, it does not mean that you do not exist.

Lost

You may not be where you want to be, but you are somewhere. When chasing after big dreams, you must measure your progress by how far you've come, not by how far you still must go. So, if your dreams are too far out of sight, be happy because that means they are big. You are not stronger than fate, but don't be too quick to judge where fate leads you. Keep moving. You may not end up where you set your sails for, but your hard work will get you to a destination that's no less great. Put your best effort forward and own it. Don't fight fate. Befriend it.

Hanging by a Thread

I tell myself that if something is meant for me, it will happen.
I believe it in my heart. Fully. But how do I spend the seconds,
minutes, and hours? How do I allow the sun to rise on me and set
on me every single day without feeling like each day is a lifetime to
get through? How do I stop the thoughts that tell me that I am the
one who is supposed to go after what I want in life? It feels like I
am stuck in one place and am not moving, like stagnant water in a
pond. I remind myself that I am a river, flowing slowly now, but one
day I will become part of the sea, or perhaps the ocean. One day I
will be crashing waves against the shore of safety, carrying ships and
hearts to the harbor.

Fate Tells Me

I tell myself that I need to stop thinking of what it is that I am waiting for. Who it is that I am waiting for to see me. That way, it will go away. They will go away. And I will be believing in fate and in what's meant to be. Who's meant to be. So I occupy myself with what's unrelated. I do what I need to do in my life on my own. And when I look back to see if what I've been waiting for is waiting for me, if whom I've been waiting for is waiting for me, and I find that I was not missed, nor was I asked about, I realize that if my absence does not awaken the beauty of my presence, then that place is not meant for me. That person is not meant for me. And that is how I tell myself what fate has been trying to tell me, but I am the one who wanted to learn on my own.

You Are What You Give

So maybe when you care, you feel that you care too much. And when you love, you drown them in your love. Maybe when you give, you give feeling like they won't understand why you're giving so much. Something reminds you that if you don't make them work for what you give them, that you, as a person, are somehow not worthy enough of being reciprocated what you already gave. Take a step back and remind yourself of this: What you give is an indication of what you own. So if you give too much care, that care comes from somewhere within you. If you love too sincerely, that love comes from somewhere within you. What you give comes from somewhere within you. That is what defines your worth; what you give and your willingness to give it knowing that you might not get anything in return, not what they take or how they take it.

The New Normal

We live in a world where you're more likely to be questioned if you're kind than you are if you're rude. It's as if rudeness has become something that we accept, or expect. But kindness makes us wonder what the person's hidden intentions are. It's deeply saddening and hypocritical that the one who chooses kindness has to question his or her intentions and wonder how others will perceive this kindness. What is even sadder is that the world has come to accept this norm. We raise our children to believe that goodness only exists in them, and the outer world is out to get them. We want to protect them, so we warn them. From our point of view, we are doing the right thing. In reality, we are setting them up to see the worst in people, and consequentially, we are scaring them away from taking risks. When we silence their vulnerability and ability to trust in others, we rob them of the beauty of connecting with other human beings.

If I Get Under Your Skin

If I get under your skin, it's probably because you hurt me. My words, you see, have no mercy on someone who causes injustice. My words have no mercy on someone who chose to hurt someone as deeply as you did. My words have no mercy on someone who had the chance to stop someone from hurting more people, and was silent about it. I have no mercy on someone who has no integrity. Someone who allows opportunity to dictate their loyalty. I am not bitter. I have just tasted the pain of being tormented by people like you who could have spoken up for me but chose to be silent. I may not be able to tell you things to your face because I am respectful, but don't you dare dictate what I can or cannot write. If I get under your skin, it's because your lack of dignity burned right through my skin and scarred my heart for eternity.

Shake It Off

I hate it when people tell me to shake a feeling off. I don't want to shake it off. I want to dive into it and understand why I am feeling it. Because if I ignore it during the day, it comes back at night. And it wakes up with me. And walks with me everywhere I go. It makes me not want to tell those people what I am feeling anymore. It makes me want to isolate myself and keep my feelings to myself. It makes me feel that there is something wrong with me for feeling the way I do. And it makes me want to conceal parts of me when all I truly want is for someone to understand me, not erase parts of me because they don't want to deal with what I feel. I am a human made of a heart and a soul that feel things very deeply. And unless someone is willing to dive into this heart and soul of mine, they might as well stay away. I no longer have interest in shallow waters.

Just One Choice

Every day, life will give you many things to choose from. You can choose to remain in your state. Or to change. You can choose to dwell on the past. Or to move toward the future. You can choose to believe in yourself. Or to be hard on yourself. You can choose to ask for more. Or to be grateful for what you have. And you don't have to decide on everything every single day. But at least make one choice. Take the lead in your life by choosing instead of giving into helplessness. With time, choice becomes a habit. If you don't know what to choose today, here is a choice that you can never go wrong with: gratitude. Be grateful for what you have, even if you feel that you deserve more. If you are not thankful for what you already have, there is no guarantee that you will be grateful for more.

Who Are You Trying to Impress?

Some people worry so much about what others think of them
that they change what they have to say to please someone else. It's
hurtful, I know, but you have to make peace with the fact that their
choice to be two-faced is their choice, not yours. We tend to put
value on those who others try to impress simply because someone
out there wants to impress them. That's how power works. Think
about it this way, though: If someone isn't impressed by the truth,
are they worthy of being impressed? If someone isn't impressed by
the truth, are they worthy of your time, effort, and energy? Are they
worthy of you trying to prove yourself to them? Are they worthy of
your mental space? No, they are not. Those who are worthy are those
who matter. And those who matter, you don't have to prove yourself
to them. They see right through you. They see your truth. They see
your authenticity. Those are the ones who are worthy of being held
on to, because you don't have to try to impress them. You already do
by being who you are.

A Castle of My Own

I crafted the doors to my castle with a chisel I sharpened with every arrow aimed at my heart. I closed these doors and hid the keys in the highest tower I built. On every step, I engraved respect. I shattered every glass window and replaced them with bars of steel. I broke down every wall tainted by the hands of those whose trustworthiness I believed in and was disappointed by. I ripped apart every paper I wrote to those who heard my words with their ears, not with their brains or hearts. I shielded my heart with a golden cage. I left the key in a dark place, and I sought the light. My soul sought peace. It sought purity from the dusty world surrounding it. It ached for the innocence within it to shine. It sought the lost key but soon realized that it did not need it, for I am already the owner of my heart.

Make a Difference

Making a difference in the world begins with making a difference in yourself. Life may pass you by, and one day you will realize that you spent years on others and always wondered when you would have time for yourself. The truth is that it is so much easier to care for others than it is to care for yourself. Honesty hurts you, but being honest with others about themselves is a lot easier. So you invest in others. You forget that the best kind of investment is in making yourself a better person. Don't stop caring for others, but promise me this: Start caring for yourself today. Let go of whatever is holding you back. No excuses. Just start.

Trust Me

It's not about who you trust. It's about what you're willing to trust people with. Even the most trustworthy of people will let out your secrets, even unintentionally. You know why? It's because no one is perfect. We are all flawed. And sometimes we underestimate our innocence and overestimate other people's innocence, so we trust with the best of intentions yet manage to come off as naive. Yes, naive, or too unrealistic. Too hopeful. Too positive. As if there could ever be too much goodness. Trust people, but don't burden them with your problems or worries. Don't trust them with things that could cage you in the past. Keep your heart on the harbor of safety. Keep your brain away from regret. Trust them with your thoughts on life, your reflections, aspirations, and values. Trust them with your manners. Trust them with your kindness. And if they betray those things, at least you've lost nothing. Instead, you will prove to yourself how strong your values are against the tides of ignorance around you.

Dream Your Journey Away

We learn a lot more from the journey than the destination. Don't focus on the result, because the fear of failure will make you blind to the possibility of success. Focus on the process instead, because it'll motivate you to take every step carefully. At least we can dream during our journey, but our destination may be scarred by reality. So enjoy your journey and push yourself to prove to yourself how capable you are of making the right decisions, of putting the right efforts forward, and of staying true to yourself.

Age and Wisdom

Respect your elders, but don't ever accept power used wrongly. Just because they're older, it doesn't mean they're wiser. Just because they're in power, it doesn't mean they're just. Just because they're accountable for their actions, it doesn't mean that they realize the importance of honesty. If you don't stand your ground, they will walk all over you and even make lies up about you if they have to keep their statuses safe. Walk with your head up high and don't look down except to remind yourself of where we all came from and where we all will end up.

Choose Beauty

People will not remember the details of what your face looks like, yet you worry the most about that. They do remember your smile. The look in your eyes while they were talking to you. The way you made them feel. How gentle you were. The comfort your words gave them and the understanding you were willing to offer. How you went out of your way to make them happy. Your kindness, your compassion, and your respectfulness. The most beautiful of faces may have the ugliest of hearts, and if that's what you're looking for, that's what you will get. But if you have a beautiful heart, your beauty will shine on people's hearts. Whether they see it or not depends on what they're looking for.

A Taste of Your Own Medicine

Don't give them a taste of their own medicine. They already know what it tastes like. Give them a taste of your own medicine. If they lied, let your medicine be honesty. If they played with your emotions, let your medicine be maturity. If they broke you, let your medicine heal. If they made you cry, let your medicine make them smile. These remedies of yours may take years to work, but they work. And they last. So be patient. Stay true to yourself. And remember this: It is better for people to value you for who you are, not for who you pretend to be. Who you are lasts a lifetime. Who you pretend to be changes like the change of seasons. Don't be afraid to be yourself, even if it means removing yourself from lives that you want to be in. You are, no doubt, worthy of being valued for who you are. So be who you are.

Listen

Stop listening to the voices around you. Focus on the voices within you. Your heart's language is the most comprehensive. Your mind's logic is the most worthy of your time. Fix yourself before you worry about fixing others. At the end of the day, no one will walk your journey for you. You have to do that. At the end of the day, no one will dream for you. You have to do that. At the end of the day, no one will lose a moment of sleep because of the sleep you lose. Learn to trust your instincts. Don't ask for advice on personal matters unless it's from family. No one has an intrinsic motive to stand up for you. If you don't want people to assume facts about you, don't assume facts about them. Teach yourself to be independent of others' opinions but respectful of them. Love solitude. Love the person that you are. Don't ever believe that you are the same as anyone else. Don't ever dare to think that being different is a crime, no matter how many people shut you out. They earned the right to be let go of. You are different, and that's a fact. You are unique, and that's a fact. Your existence is in your hands, so let it shine. Let it inspire. Let it be free.

Understand Me

Would you ask the sun why it shines brighter on some days than others? Would you ask the moon why it breaks the darkness on some nights and not others? Such is the course of life. Some days, we give our best, but other days, we just exist. Some days, we are kings and queens of our minds and souls, and some days, we are slaves to our hearts. So much within us is easy to misjudge if it is not understood. And people are more likely to misjudge us than to try to understand us.

The Best in Me

You should never be afraid to say: *If you're not living my life, don't think you know how I should live it.* Unfortunately, many people out there don't understand that your life is different than theirs. That your priorities are different than theirs. That your definition of *right* and *wrong* may be different than theirs, and they don't understand that that's completely normal. So, as long as you believe in yourself, zone them out. It is so easy to judge a person's decisions if we don't try to understand the reasons that led to those decisions. So, if they don't try to understand you and assume the best, they will assume the worst and, therefore, do not belong in your life. Gravitate toward those who assume the best in you, even at your worst.

Doors Unlocked

Not every door that comes your way is worthy of being unlocked. The handles on some doors will break before you even turn your key. And sometimes, you try so hard to use the keys that you have to unlock the wrong doors that they break or get stuck . . . and the doors that you were meant to open stay closed for you to regret and wonder about the happiness that could have been hidden behind them.

Change

I believe in goodness. I believe in good intentions. I believe in a power stronger than any kind of willpower we may think we have. We are destined to make mistakes. We are destined to be flawed. Each and every one of us. No one is perfect. We all lie sometimes. We all allow our hearts to dip into temptation sometimes. Sometimes we judge, and sometimes we make promises we can't keep. Sometimes we walk down paths knowing they are dead ends before we even take the first step, and sometimes we turn away from the roads that promise us happiness out of fear. We all make mistakes, and the fact that we make them differently does not lessen the importance of reflecting upon them and making them better. If you believe that the world can change, you must believe that you must change. So go ahead. Start.

A Sunset You Dread

The sun doesn't always rise at the same time or set at the same time, but we are always certain that it will happen at the perfect time. Have faith that everything will work out the way it should at the right time. Don't just think of yourself but think of the grand scheme of things. Think of those who waited for the sunrise for you, even if, by doing so, it means that you are expecting a sunset. Be thankful for patience, for persistence, and for good intentions.

It's Not You

When you don't get what you want, you quickly assume that it's because you don't deserve it or because you are not worthy enough to get it. But have you ever thought that it could be because it doesn't deserve you or because it is not worthy of you? The truth is that we always give ourselves less credit than we deserve. And sometimes, many times, we live in denial of what we really deserve, so we settle for what is less. There is a power much higher than us, much wiser than us, that is willing to crush our feelings sometimes so it can open our eyes to the strength that we have inside and to the reality of what we truly deserve.

Let Go

They say that, at some point, you just learn to let go. I must disagree. If it just takes one moment to let go, then you never really held on tightly enough. To a dream. To a goal. To a place. To a person. To anything. I believe that you let go little by little. You let go a little, then hold back on, but with a little less force until you fully release yourself. And the tighter you hold on, the more force you let go with. The deeper you dive, the higher you'll fly. The closer you get, the further you'll pull away. The weaker you feel, the stronger you'll become. So do not be ashamed of your weaknesses. We all have them. You must learn to be kind to yourself. You must learn to understand yourself. You must believe in yourself. Never think that you are a bad person. Differentiate between your self-worth and your actions. To say that you are bad is different than saying that you made a mistake. You can't fix yourself, but you can fix a mistake. And remember, not one person on this earth is perfect. We all make mistakes. We all fall. We all have flaws. We just need to look within ourselves and treat ourselves as humans who are worthy of respect and hope. Do not give up on yourself. Get back up. Be brave. Be happy.

Clarity

You may wait for a sunrise that may never come. You may ignore the thought of an inevitable sunset. You may anticipate an opportunity in front of a closed door. You may wait for a chance that will never be given to you. You may wait. You may see what does not exist, and you may be completely blind to what does. Your vision may be shut down by your hopes, and it may be blurred by what you think you deserve. You may wish. You may hope. You may pray. You may wonder why your understanding and perception of reality could be so wrong at times. At the end of the day, your thoughts keep you wondering. Your realizations keep you reflecting and learning. Your mistakes keep you growing. After all, your own perception of reality is nothing but a reflection of what you want your reality to be. You don't always smile when you're happy, and sometimes, when every piece of you is urging you to relieve it with an expression of anger, you choose to be calm. At your weakest moments, the strength you display can be more convincing than strength itself. It's a matter of choice. It's a matter of believing in a power much higher than you that can lead you in the right direction even if you can't see where you are stepping. It's a matter of consciously doing what is right rather than only refraining from what is wrong. Goodness is a choice. It is not the default. It is not easy. Life will put you on pathways to test your resilience. Will you settle for believing that being sincere is a weakness? Will you settle for believing that being honest is wrong? Will you leave a piece of your soul with every person and every place that disappointed you? Or, will you collect those pieces and put them back together with the spirit of faith and make your soul a beautiful mosaic of pieces that dared to fall and get back up even stronger? Pieces that dared to be left than to leave, to be hurt by others than to hurt others, to wait than to make others wait, to be disappointed than to disappoint? If you do not believe in people, how will you empower them? How will you learn? How will you become strong? How will you heal if you do not break? If you do not believe that the cure is coming, and that only time can bring it, how will you heal? Would the thirsty bits of the earth ever reject rain after its absence? You see, we really are a distortion ourselves, yet we expect reality to be so clear.

Choose

Today, I choose to be happy. I choose to let go. I choose to be myself. To love myself. To cherish myself. Today, I choose to let go of the people whose company is toxic to my peace of mind. Today, I choose to be free. I choose to liberate my soul from the aches it's been through. Today, I choose to stay away from closed doors. I choose not to craft a wall around my heart. I choose to decorate it with the lessons I've learned. I choose to paint it with respect and confidence. Today, I choose to forgive myself. For being too much of myself. For allowing myself to hurt myself. Today, I choose to embrace my flaws. I choose to accept my mistakes. Today, I choose to change. I choose to be better. I choose to move forward. I choose to guard my soul. Today, I choose to be brave. I choose to say no when saying yes hurts. Today, I choose to be wise. I choose to walk away from places I don't belong. I choose to embrace my time. For all that is timeless is precious. All that is precious is unique. All that is unique is different. And all that is different is beautiful. Today, I choose to be beautiful.

Acknowledgments

Thank you
for walking this journey with me,
for making space for my words in your heart,
for honoring my voice, for honoring my heart,
for honoring your voice, for honoring your heart.

And thank you, my mother,
for seeing me through your eyes.
There is no better version of myself
than the one you see.

About the Author

Najwa Zebian is a Lebanese-Canadian author, speaker, and educator. Her passion for language was evident from a young age, as she delved into Arabic poetry and novels. The search for a home—what Najwa describes as a place where the soul and heart feel at peace—was central to her early years. When she arrived in Canada at the age of sixteen, she felt unstable and adrift in an unfamiliar place. Nevertheless, she completed her education and went on to become a teacher as well as a doctoral candidate in educational leadership. Her first students, a group of young refugees, led her back to her original passion: writing. She began to heal her sixteen-year-old self by writing to heal her students. Since self-publishing her first collection of poetry and prose in 2016, Najwa has become an inspiration to millions of people worldwide. Drawing on her own experiences of displacement, discrimination, and abuse, Najwa uses her words to encourage others to build a home within themselves; to live, love, and create fearlessly.

Instagram   **Twitter**   **Facebook**   **YouTube**
@najwazebian   @najwazebian   @najwazebian1   youtube.com/najwazebian

MIND PLATTER

Andrews McMeel Publishing
a division of Andrews McMeel Universal
1130 Walnut Street, Kansas City, Missouri 64106

www.andrewsmcmeel.com

18 19 20 21 22 BVG 10 9 8 7 6 5 4 3 2 1

ISBN: 978-1-4494-9287-8

Library of Congress Control Number: 2017962582

Editor: Melissa Rhodes
Art Director: Holly Swayne
Production Editor: Elizabeth A. Garcia
Production Manager: Cliff Koehler

Cover illustration by Wajeha Chams
Author photo by Saleme Fayad Photography

ATTENTION: SCHOOLS AND BUSINESSES
Andrews McMeel books are available at quantity discounts with bulk purchase
for educational, business, or sales promotional use. For information,
please e-mail the Andrews McMeel Publishing Special Sales Department:
specialsales@amuniversal.com.